THE OTHER HALF

First published in Australia in 2006 by
New Holland Publishers (Australia) Pty Ltd
Sydney • Auckland • London • Cape Town
14 Aquatic Drive Frenchs Forest NSW 2086 Australia
218 Lake Road Northcote Auckland New Zealand
86 Edgware Road London W2 2EA United Kingdom
80 McKenzie Street Cape Town 8001 South Africa

National Library of Australia cataloguing in publication data
Clarke, Lliane.
      The other half : extraordinary women and life, love and famous partners.
      ISBN 1 74110 452 1.
      1. Celebrities - Biography. 2. Women - Biography. 3.
      Marriages of celebrities. I. Title.

    920.72

Publisher: Martin Ford
Project Editor: Lliane Clarke
Designer: Leigh Nankervis
Production Manager: Linda Bottari
Printer: Tien Wah Press (S'pore) Pte Ltd

10 9 8 7 6 5 4 3 2 1

The Other Half

EXTRAORDINARY WOMEN AND LIFE, LOVE AND FAMOUS PARTNERS

LLIANE CLARKE
AND GERALDINE COREN, EMMA DRIVER, FRANCESCA FORD
AMANDA GOFF AND MICHAEL MCGRATH

NEW HOLLAND

Contents

Introduction

'It hasn't been easy going. I'm still not clear ... I feel in that sense it's more than what's known as a double load. That is to say, if I were Lee Krasner but had never married Jackson Pollock would I have had the same experience I have being Mrs Jackson Pollock?'

LEE KRASNER

So MANY FAMOUS MEN begin their award acceptance speeches saying, 'Thanks. But really I couldn't have done it without my other half!' And most of the time they couldn't. Their wives and partners supported, encouraged, backed, financed, mothered and loved them on their road to success.

The Other Half looks at the women who didn't stay in the background administering support. These women stepped out and took some fame for themselves. They used, took advantage of, grabbed, welcomed, bathed in, and in some cases were dragged into, the light of fame. Many became even more successful than their partners and live on in our memories long after their partners have faded.

All these women married or partnered someone who was famous, someone who changed the way we live in or look at the world. Would they have been happy if they had married a train driver or school teacher? How much did they want to marry someone famous? Did they marry to promote their own talents? Was power an aphrodisiac in their marriage?

Discovering these women's lives from the perspective of the twenty-first century is a revelation. For example, *Frankenstein's* author Mary Shelley was born only 20 years after French Queen Marie Antoinette, yet Mary's bohemian life of travel and bisexuality seems centuries older than the doomed queen rustling in long skirts along the corridors of the Palace of Versailles. Has Mary's book outlived Percy Shelley's poetry? Who can remember the name of Marie's husband?

Living under the harsh glare of publicity can be uncomfortable. When Jacqueline Kennedy-Onassis witnessed the murder of her first husband, the whole world watched too. And double doses of fame bring with them alienation from the rest of the world. When Crown Princess Mary married into royalty she accepted that role. Priscilla Presley found herself there at an early age. Yet many women broke out of that cage and reinvented their own future. Tina Turner escaped her violent but famous relationship with Ike, which on the outside looked like a nice place to be.

Fame demands time—for work, travel, interviews and promotion. How does a relationship cope on minimum time and a double load of fame? These women's marriages are certainly not your average domestic arrangement. What was it like for Frida Kahlo to be married to a volatile artist like Diego Rivera, or for Jacqueline Kennedy to survive her charismatic and powerful husband John F Kennedy? How did these women's children fare?

Fame brings with it a fear of mediocrity and a quest for adoration. This pressure leads to increased chances of extra marital affairs. Diana, Princess of Wales famously stated: 'There are three people in this marriage', and she wasn't wrong. Yet many women haven't left this particular trapping of fame to the men. Elizabeth Taylor was almost as famous for her acting as her multiple marriages. Paula Yates' profile only increased with her second famous husband, Michael Hutchence. Many commentators pass over Simone de Beauvoir's books and concentrate on the details of her 'open relationship'.

Many women have found themselves famous by accident, particularly in the world of politics. Winnie Mandela had to speak for her husband for so long as he lay in prison, some suggest she lost her own voice on the way. Cory Aquino and Sirimavo Bandaranaike were thrust into their national leadership roles when their husbands were assassinated. Hillary Rodham-Clinton has taken a different tack, and now directs her own political career.

While many of these women's lives have been turned into books and films, the women have added to their own myths as well, deliberately blurring the facts of their own lives. Several have hidden as much as they can from the media. Lee Krasner's motivation and persona differ depending on who you read. Annita Keating shuns the Australian media, releasing only tantalising comments about her life with the former Australian prime minister. Sharon Arden-Osbourne is a clever media manipulator. The self-promotion of Imelda Marcos has meant a lot of her stories about herself are contradictory.

All women battle against assumptions about what a female can do. Apart from fascination, it's difficult not to feel admiration for the life these women managed to achieve in their lifetime, alongside their ambitious and often self-obsessed partners. Perhaps these women needed their famous husbands to get them to the top.

Perhaps they didn't.

LLIANE CLARKE

Lee Krasner quote from *Three Artists*, by Anne Middleton Wagner, University of California Press.

Breaking New Ground
1750-1899

Marie Antoinette

Was the beautiful Austrian princess and Queen of France, Marie Antoinette, a tragic victim of circumstance, or was she indeed the epitome of decadence? Did she really say 'let them eat cake'? As she finally stepped up to the guillotine, she secured a place in history that would resonate for far longer than her husband's.

MARIE ANTOINETTE was the fifteenth daughter of Marie Thérèse, Empress of Austria. She was born in 1755 in Vienna and was raised as a princess amongst wealth and privilege in the Hapsburg House of Austria, the oldest royal house of Europe.

Some say that Marie Antoinette was bred to be used as a bargaining chip in the Franco-Austrian alliance. Certainly, Marie Thérèse was proud of her ability to marry off her many children in ways that would strengthen her Austrian empire. For her pretty young daughter, Marie Antoinette, said to be her favourite, Marie Thérèse arranged a marriage with the son of the French king, Louis XV.

When she married the young Louis in 1770, Marie Antoinette was 15 years old, her groom 16. When the old king died and her husband became King Louis XVI in 1774, Marie Antoinette, aged 19, became Queen of France.

Louis XVI (1754–1793) was young and unprepared to govern, his elder brother having died prematurely. The new monarch's loyalty and sense of duty were mediocre. He was said to lack any personal presence and decisiveness—characteristics that eventually led to the demise of the French monarchy. Louis was homely, awkward, keen on hunting and clocks. The graceful and beautiful teenager he had married, on the other hand, was passionate about the arts, fashion, dance and French nightlife.

The French people supported their King, but were suspicious of his foreign Queen. Marie Antoinette's lack of popularity was not helped by a delay of 11 years in producing a royal heir— Louis was unable to achieve an erection. Their marriage was said to be unconsummated for seven years. It took the intervention of Marie Antoinette's oldest brother, Emperor Joseph of Austria, in

Archduke Maximilian Franz visits Marie Antoinette and Louis XVI.

a heart-to-heart meeting with Louis in 1777, to convince him to have a necessary operation.

Louis XVI officially charged Marie Antoinette with entertaining his court. Her efforts made a real impact: grand balls were held once again, the number of theatres in Paris grew, and there was a radical change in both musical and theatrical repertories. For several reasons—escape from her marital frustration, the boredom of court life, and a desire to recreate her childhood—Marie Antoinette surrounded herself with a close group of friends. She lavished expensive gifts and positions on them and often ignored her obligations towards to the great houses of the French nobility—a social error which would prove to be fatal.

Marie Antoinette found ways to express her individuality outside the close confines of the royal household at Versailles. She hired an architect to design a little pavilion where she and her friends could escape from court life. Adjacent to this Petit Trianon, she commissioned Le Hameau, an artificially constructed medieval village. Here Marie and her friends would dress up and imitate a rustic village life, acting out, it was rumoured, sexual fantasies of peasant life.

In the late 1780s there was a growing resentment among the public and French nobility of Marie Antoinette's influence over the King and her public display of extravagance. Some stories were true stories and some were fabricated.

The Queen's extravagance, dissipation and sexual exploits were highlighted by the 'diamond necklace affair', which grabbed the attention of the entire nation. An impoverished aristocrat, Madame de Lamotte, had been scheming for years to gain a position at the royal court. At the same time the Cardinal of France, Prince de Rohan, was unhappy over his exclusion from Marie Antoinette's inner circle. Boehmer, a jeweller, was also trying to convince Marie Antoinette to buy an expensive diamond necklace.

Lamotte convinced the Cardinal that she was a lesbian lover of Marie Antoinette and that the Queen wanted Boehmer's necklace. The Cardinal obtained the necklace from Boehmer and gave it to Lamotte, after meeting a prostitute dressed as Marie Antoinette at a late night rendezvous. When Boehmer approached the Queen for payment, Lamotte's plot unravelled. The King and Queen were outraged that he would think that the Queen would trade sexual favours for a necklace, and the Cardinal was arrested. The Queen demanded public vindication, so the King ordered a trial before the Parlement of Paris, with the Cardinal charged with insulting the Queen. The Parlement of Nobles acquitted the Cardinal of the charge and said that at the least, given her reputation, the Queen was worthy of such insult. When the not guilty verdict was announced, a shocked Marie Antoinette rushed to her coach, amid a jeering crowd.

In 1778, Marie Antoinette gave birth to the first of four children—Marie Thérèse, or 'Madame Royale'—and to the first Dauphin in 1781. She had another daughter, who died in infancy, and another son in 1785. Her image improved with her motherhood. The French nation, however, was struggling from bad harvests in the late 1780s and the peasants were starving. Marie's perceived callousness led many to believe she said 'Let them eat cake', when told of the lack of bread. This remark set her fame in stone and has remained in usage for over 220 years. Its authenticity, however, is still hotly debated.

France was also reeling under huge debts. Amid the grief of losing two children (including their oldest son and heir, who died of consumption, aged seven), and unable to force the nobility to make needed financial reforms, the desperate King Louis called an Estates General in May 1789. This forum gave representation to the public, but the common people were not content with their limited role. The third estate declared itself the national assembly and in the 'Tennis Court Oath' said it would not adjourn until France had a constitution.

Louis lacked the will to quell this rebellion and was repeatedly lobbied to take action by Marie Antoinette. After the storming of the Bastille and the Declaration of the Rights of Man, on October 4, Louis and Marie were forcibly taken from Versailles to the Tuileries Palace in Paris. Marie Antoinette appealed for help from other European rulers, including her brother, the Austrian Emperor, and convinced the reluctant Louis to flee France.

The Queen's friend and rumoured lover, Axel Fersen, arranged a coach. The royal couple and their children, all disguised as common travellers, escaped from Paris. But the King and Queen had insisted on all their comforts, so their coach was lumbering and slow, and spotted by one Jacques Drouet. He noticed an attractive but familiar-looking woman who issued orders, even though she was dressed as a maid, and from a gold piece given as a tip, recognised the King. Drouet sped ahead and alerted the people of Varennes. The King and Queen were forced to return to Paris.

In December 1792, King Louis XVI was summoned before the National Convention and tried for treason. He was convicted and sentenced to death and in 1793 was executed on the guillotine. Soon afterwards, the now thin and pallid Marie Antoinette was awoken at night to face the Revolutionary Tribunal. Like her husband, Marie was found guilty.

When she rode to her death on 16 October 1793, Marie Antoinette was 38. The crowd saw an old hag in peasant clothes, with roughly shorn hair—a stark contrast to the elegant and voluptuous Queen. She sat straight and tried to retain her dignity as she rode in the garbage cart amid the crowd's whistles and jeers.

After she was beheaded, her head was throne in the cart between her legs and her body left on the grass before being dumped in an unmarked grave. So ended the life of once the most illustrious and glamourous woman in all of Europe.

Abigail Adams

*The wife and mother of two American presidents, Abigail Adams'
enduring legacy has been her writings about political and domestic life
in colonial, revolutionary and early post-revolutionary America. She is
remembered for her opposition to slavery and as an early advocate for
women's rights.*

ABIGAIL SMITH was born in 1744 in Weymouth, Massachusetts, to William Smith and Elizabeth Quincy, both from well-respected New England families. Like most girls of her time, Abigail was denied a formal education—which frustrated her in her adult life and fuelled her passionate belief in full education for girls.

Abigail was encouraged by her minister father to use his large library, however, and from an early age she became an avid reader. She met Harvard graduate John Adams at her sister's wedding in 1759, when she was just 15 and John a 27-year-old lawyer. This initial meeting was followed by another two years later when the pair fell in love.

Their letters document a 54-year marriage based on passionate love, mutual respect and intellectual compatibility. Abigail thought of John as her 'dearest friend', and John more than once acknowledged that without his wife's support his achievements in public life would not have been possible. After their marriage in October 1764, the couple set up home in Braintree (later Quincy), Massachusetts. In the first ten years of their marriage, Abigail gave birth to six children, four of whom survived. While John's work, first as a lawyer then as politician and diplomat, regularly required him to travel, she stayed at home managing the household, farm and family.

Abigail did not question her role and saw it as a wife's duty to manage the 'home front', smoothing the path for her husband's success. John became a leader of the American Revolution, a founding father who helped design the United States Constitution. As John's work-related absences increased, Abigail became a decisive and enterprising administrator of her family's affairs.

While she didn't champion votes for women, Abigail was committed to education for women, for women to have a major contribution to educating and rearing their children, and for women to manage household affairs. She also spoke out about women's property rights.

In 1776, John was in Philadelphia helping Congress draft laws designed to enshrine the right to independence. Abigail appealed to him in one of her most famous letters: 'Remember the Ladies,' she wrote, 'and be more generous and favourable to them than your ancestors. Do not put such unlimited power into the hands of the Husbands. Remember all Men would be tyrants if they could. If particular care and attention is not paid to the Ladies we are determined to foment a Rebellion, and will not hold ourselves bound by any Laws in which we have no voice, or Representation.'

> *'Do not put such unlimited power into the hands of the Husbands. Remember all Men would be tyrants if they could.'*

Abigail's voice was among the first to question the position of women and stimulated the historic movement towards universal suffrage and equal rights. In the nation's formative years, hers was a voice calling for a deeper appreciation of the role of women. There was no women's movement as such—not even a suffragette movement—at this early time, only the occasional, isolated voice of women such as Abigail and her friend Mercy Otis Warren, who had the ear of their ruling class male peers.

In the years 1784-88, Abigail accompanied her husband on diplomatic missions to France and England. On their return, the couple's long separations continued as he served as the first Vice President of the United States (1789–97) and then as President (1797–1801). John's reliance on Abigail for counsel during his presidency is evident in his description of his wife as his 'fellow labourer.'

After John's term as President ended, the couple returned to Quincy in 1801. Abigail died in October 1818 of typhoid fever, seven years before her son, John Quincy Adams, became the sixth president of the United States. John Adams died in 1826.

Much of the recognition of Abigail as an advocate for human rights has been understood retrospectively, in light of historical developments, although the fact that at the time John Adams' opponents believed she had too much influence on the President suggests that her powers of persuasion were well known before her letters became public. Hers is a classic tale of 'the woman behind the man', as this was the only model then in existence. Her political lobbying took the form of persuading her husband personally.

Most of Abigail Adams's correspondence is held at the Massachusetts Historical Society. Her opinionated letters to her husband, friends and family have been collected in many anthologies since the 19th century. The largest published collection of her letters is contained in *The Adams Papers: Adams Family Correspondence*, edited by L H Butterfield.

Mary Shelley

The author of Frankenstein *lived in the shadow of her poet husband Percy while they were alive, but her novel, and its countless movie adaptations, remains as a lasting icon.*

MARY WOLLSTONECRAFT GODWIN was born in 1797 into English literary celebrity—the child of an academic and socially-committed family in London. She was the only daughter of William Godwin, a writer best known for his philosophical work *Political Justice*, and his novel *Caleb Williams*. Author and feminist Mary Wollstonecraft, who wrote *Vindication of the Rights of Women*, was her mother.

Tragically, her mother died ten days after Mary was born. Her father then married Mary Jane Clairmont, who had a daughter he hoped would be company for Mary. While Mary was close to the younger Jane, her relationship with her stepmother was strained. The new Mrs Godwin resented Mary's intense affection for her father and was jealous of the special interest visitors showed in the product of the union between the two most radical thinkers of the day.

Mary grew up in London in her father's intellectual circle, which included literary giants like William Wordsworth, Charles Lamb, Samuel Taylor Coleridge and William Hazlitt. She said her favourite pastime was to 'write stories' that had 'creations far more interesting to me than my own sensations'.

Mary first met Percy Bysshe Shelley in 1812, when she was 14. She met him again when he was estranged from his wife, Harriet Westbrook Shelley. He came from an aristocratic background, had a private income and had received his education at Eton and briefly at Oxford. Before the age of 17, he had already published two Gothic romances.

When she was 16, Mary eloped with Shelley, to avoid her father's disapproval, and travelled through France and Switzerland. They were accompanied by her step-sister Jane Clairmont, or 'Claire', with whom they both had an intense and personal relationship. Their household was one that experimented with 'free love' and Claire was much more than a step-sister.

In 1815, aged 17, Mary had the first of many pregnancies and gave birth to a premature child who died. The threesome settled for a while in Windsor, outside London. The next year Mary gave birth to William. They were a restless family, spirits on the move for inspiration and subject matter. When William was four months old, they left for Geneva, with Claire, to meet up with their friend the writer Lord Byron.

They spent the summer of 1816 with Byron in Geneva, reading, writing, discussing a wide range of topics and boating on the lake. It was a particularly wet summer, and they were confined to the house for days due to heavy rain, crowded around a raging fire. Their topics ranged from Greek mythology to new scientific inventions, particularly electricity.

'Many and long were the conversations between Lord Byron and Shelley, to which I was a devout but nearly silent listener,' Mary says. 'During one of these, various philosophical doctrines were discussed and among others the nature of the principle of life and whether there was any probability of this ever being discovered and communicated.'

One night Lord Byron announced that 'we will each write a ghost story'. Mary went to bed that night but couldn't sleep. 'My imagination, unbidden, possessed and guided me. I saw the hideous phantasm of a man stretched out and then, on the working of some powerful engine, show signs of life, and stir with an uneasy half vital motion,' she writes. The next morning she woke up and rushed to write down the 'grim terrors' of her dream.

Her contribution was *Frankenstein* (subtitled *The Modern Prometheus*), a story about a student of natural philosophy who learns the secret of imparting life to a creature constructed from bones he has collected. It is not just a study of the macabre and has many interpretations; some critics say it is about creativity itself, and its potential to destroy its disciples. Others say it is a study of how man uses his power, through science, to manipulate and pervert his own destiny.

She later looked back on the 'happy days, when death and grief were but words, which found no true echo in my heart'.

Byron wrote the poem 'Prometheus' in that summer of 1816, and a vampire story, and Shelley wrote *Prometheus Unbound* (published in 1820), but they didn't match the drama of Mary's monster story, which she continued to develop, on Shelley's insistence. Its concentric structure, with three stories within one, remains completely original.

Her book was virtually complete when, in that same year, 1816, Shelley's first wife Harriet committed suicide. Mary and Shelley were then free to marry, which they did in London and moved back to England. In 1817 Mary completed *Frankenstein* and their daughter Clara was born.

Mary says in her Introduction to *Frankenstein* that 'my husband was from the very first, anxious that I should prove myself worthy of my parentage and enrol myself on the page of fame. He desired that I should write, not so much with the idea that I could produce anything worthy of notice, but that he might himself judge how far I possessed the promise of better things hereafter.'

Frankenstein was turned down by two publishers before it was finally published in three volumes in 1818 by Lackington, Allen & Company in London, written by 'Anonymous'. Mary, Percy, Claire and the two children left for Italy and settled in Bagni di Lucca.

They visited Lord Byron in Venice, but here baby Clara became ill and died of dysentery. They journeyed south and settled in the warmer Naples for the winter. Illness was never far from the family and in 1819, while in Rome, young William died of malaria. They moved to Florence, as Mary was pregnant again. There, Percy Florence was born. Meanwhile in London the identity of the anonymous author of *Frankenstein* was becoming common knowledge. A few years after the book was first published, it was translated to the stage.

The family kept up a relentless travelling agenda. They moved to Pisa and settled in a village near Lerici on the Italian Riviera. Byron visited and they lived happily for a short time. Mary was aware of Shelley's affairs with other women, but trusted that time would bring them together. Time was not on her side. Tragedy struck in 1822. While sailing to Leghorn, Percy Shelley was drowned.

Devastated by Shelley's death, Mary returned to London with Percy Florence in 1823. She later looked back on the 'happy days, when death and grief were but words, which found no true echo in my heart'. She was just 26 and had lived through the deaths of three children and her husband, a creative relationship with two of the century's great poets, and had written her own novel and another book, *History of a Six Weeks' Tour*.

In London, Mary threw herself into her work as editor and writer. Committing herself to the immortalisation of her husband, she decided to write his biography and publish a definitive collection of his poems. Later she created an idealised portrait of him in her novel, *The Last Man* (1826). Her desire to glorify Percy was blocked, however, by his father, Sir Timothy Shelley, who was embarrassed by any public mention of his revolutionary and atheistic son. Mary contented herself with appending long biographical notes to her 1824 and 1839 editions of his poetry.

Despite the book's success and the fact her son was in line to inherit the Shelley family wealth, Mary had little money. Even so, she managed to send Percy Florence to Harrow School and Cambridge University and travel with him through Europe. She wrote and published *Perkin Warbeck*, *Lodore*, *Rambles in Germany and Italy*, and *Falkner*, her last novel.

In 1844 Shelley's father died and left Percy Florence the estate. For a short time Mary lived a little more comfortably. She died of a brain tumour in 1851, aged 54, and was buried at Bournemouth. *Frankenstein* has appeared in numerous editions and translations all over the world. In the 1930s it became a blockbuster Hollywood film, starring Boris Karloff. The movie propelled the story and its creator into modern legend.

Bertha Benz

The first person to drive a car over any distance was Bertha Benz, the wife of its inventor Karl Benz. Her determination shaped the history of the modern motor car. Without her, it may have taken a different turn and the Mercedes-Benz corporation could have died in its infancy.

Bertha Ringer was born in Pforzheim, Germany on 3 May 1849. In her teens, she met and became engaged to Karl Benz, the son of an engine driver, five years her junior.

Karl had just started his own company, supplying building materials. But he was in a difficult financial situation with this business partner. To solve what she saw as a gridlock, and to release her fiancé from financial burden, Bertha paid out the partner with her wedding dowry. From then on Karl had power over his own business.

Bertha married Karl in 1872 when she was 23. Over the next decade, she gave birth to five children. Despite the domestic burden, Bertha was always interested in, and was never far from, her husband's business.

Karl became an inventor and design engineer, but he often suffered serious technical setbacks. This would fuel his increasing doubts about the direction his life's work was taking. Bertha was the eternal optimist. She encouraged, cajoled and pushed him to continue his work on engine-powered transport.

Karl started Benz & Co in 1883 in Mannheim to produce industrial engines. It was there that he invented and patented various two-stroke engines, and heard about Gottlieb Daimler, who was working on a four-wheeled vehicle. Daimler inspired Karl and he started working on his own *motorwagen*, with a four-stroke engine.

Benz was not just an engine designer. As well as the engine (which was a single-cylinder, water-cooled, 0.75 hp unit), he designed the whole vehicle. In 1886 Karl applied for a patent for his three-wheeled automobile with its gas engine. The patent specification (DRP. No. 37435) is recognised today as the birth certificate of the automobile.

However, here the motor revolution stalled. Although the public were interested in the *motorwagen*, it was not a commercial success because people didn't believe it would work. Horse power was still seen as a safer and more reliable option. Karl was plagued by self-doubt. Bertha

reasoned that the only way to convince people that the motor car would actually work was to prove it to them in practice.

'People only buy what they know,' Bertha apparently told him. 'First you must show them your wares, then they will jump at the opportunity.'

Bertha's determination led her on an historic journey. One morning in August 1888, Bertha Benz, then aged 39, and her sons Eugen, aged 15, and Richard, aged 14, started up the three-wheeled Patent Motor Car (model no. 3) in Mannheim without telling her husband what they were going to do.

> *Bertha Benz is now credited with being the 'mother of the automobile'*
> *and the first person to have driven a motorcar over any distance.*

The trio then set out on the first long-distance journey in automotive history, heading for Pforzheim, some 60 kilometres away, to visit relatives, a hazardous trip on dirt roads. Bertha wanted to prove her husband's invention did work and that people could move around without the use of horses. At the time, there were no car workshops or petrol stations. Hence the pharmacy in the town of Wiesloch became the world's first filling station. Pharmacies were the only places where gasoline, called ligroin and serving purely medical purposes at the time, was available.

The journey tested Bertha's ingenuity and determination. A blacksmith repaired a torn drive chain, and the brake pads had to be replaced several times. Bertha's hat pin apparently came in handy for unclogging the fuel lines.

Bertha and her two boys arrived in Pforzheim late at night. They sent Karl a telegram about the successful completion of the long-distance journey.

News of this sensational event spread like wildfire, and the critics were won over by the reliability of the Benz motor car. Karl Benz was later to write in his memoirs: 'Only one person stood by me during those times when I was heading towards the abyss. That was my wife. With her bravery and courage she could always find new hope.'

Bertha Benz is now credited with being the Mother of the Automobile and the first person to have driven a motorcar over any distance.

In 1903 Benz retired from Benz & Co, but he remained a member of the supervisory board until his death. The Benz and Daimler firms merged to form Daimler-Benz in 1926—the company's cars have since been called Mercedes-Benz, and Daimler.

Karl died in 1929. Bertha lived for nearly 20 more years and died in 1944, two days after celebrating her 95th birthday in Ladenburg, in the state of Baden, where the family had finally settled.

A New Century Turns
1900-1919

Alma Schindler

Alma Schindler was muse, wife and lover to some of the greatest artists of the twentieth century—Gustav Klimt, Oskar Kokoshka, Gustav Mahler, Walter Gropius, Franz Werfel. Was she a frustrated artist, a headhunter of geniuses, or the ultimate femme fatale?

ALMA MARIA SCHINDLER was born in 1879 in Vienna, the capital of the Austro-Hungarian Empire, into an artistic family. Her father, Jakob Schindler, was a successful landscape painter. Her mother, Anna von Bergen, was a German singer. Their home was open to the artists and performers of Vienna. At the turn of the century, this city was the birthplace of modernism in the arts in virtually every sphere. And Alma Schindler was right in the middle of it.

'I want to do something really remarkable,' she wrote in her *Diary of 1898–1902*, published by Cornell University. 'Would like to compose a really good opera—something no woman has ever achieved … Please God, give me some great mission, give me something great to do!'

The artist Gustav Klimt was a regular visitor to the house. He was taken with Alma's beauty, her sculptural features and fair skin, and was reputed to be the first main to kiss her. In her diary she wrote: 'On St. Mark's Square, Klimt asked me: "Alma, you'll keep a tiny spot in your heart for me—for ever—won't you, Alma?" And I replied: "For ever." He really understood women. He didn't demand my whole heart. He knew: sooner or later it would belong to someone else.'

Jakob Schindler was at the height of his career when he died in 1892. Alma was only 13. Grieving for her husband, Anna continued to support Alma's education, by engaging tutors. Vienna Burgtheater director Max Burckhard encouraged her natural interest in classical and modern literature. Composer Alexander Zemlinsky was engaged as her composition tutor, also introducing her to the ground-breaking classical composer Arnold Schoenberg.

Zemlinsky became Alma's first lover. Under his tuition she began composing *Lieder* and instrumental pieces and began an opera. In 1900 Zemlinsky's opera *Es war einmal* (Once Upon a Time) premiered at the Vienna Court Opera, under the musical direction of Gustav Mahler. A composer and conductor, Gustav Mahler also held one of the most powerful positions in the Viennese music scene—Director of the Royal Opera.

Alma had an intense attraction to creative artists. When she met Mahler in 1901 she was immediately attracted. 'Met Mahler … I must say I like him immensely—although he's dreadfully restless,' she wrote in her diary. 'He stormed about the room like a savage. The fellow is made entirely of oxygen. When you approach him, you get burnt.'

By December that year they were engaged. Mahler was 20 years older than Alma, a fact that Sigmund Freud would later point out to Gustav put him in her subconscious as a father substitute. At the age of 22, Alma left a devastated Zemlinsky. She had her own artistic aspirations and wanted to compose music. But it was a mistake to think that Mahler would support her in her career.

In March 1902, Alma married Mahler in Vienna and toured with him as he conducted the world premier of his *Third Symphony*. Maria Anna was born that year. Mahler wrote to Alma: 'The role of composer falls to me, yours is that of loving companion …' She obeyed him, reluctantly, but supported him emotionally and ran the house while he worked. In 1904 their second child, Anna Maria, was born.

In 1907 tragedy struck when Maria Anna died aged five. Alma suffered a nervous breakdown and Gustav at this time developed acute heart problems. A power feud at the Vienna Court Opera saw Mahler sever his contract and conduct there for the last time. Whether it was to leave their tragedy behind, or to escape the politics of the Vienna Court Opera, the Mahlers travelled to New York in 1908. Gustav conducted at the New York Metropolitan Opera and embarked on a concert tour, but when Alma suffered an 'unspecified illness' they returned to Austria for the summer.

After eight years of marriage to Mahler, Alma was frustrated by the lack of outlet for her own creativity. She sought consolation in the arms of the young architect Walter Gropius, who she met in 1910 while 'taking the waters' in Tobelbad in Austria. Sensing the crisis in their marriage, Mahler began to take an interest in her composition and had five of her *Lieder* printed. But it was too late, as she said in her memoirs: 'Ten years of wasted development cannot be made up anymore. It was a galvanised corpse that he wanted to resurrect.'

Back in New York, Mahler fell ill with slow endocarditis. By 1911 he was facing death. Alma sailed with him from New York back to Europe, where he died in Vienna in 1911 and was buried with his daughter Maria Anna.

Alma was still corresponding with Walter Gropius while World War I raged across Europe, and refused a marriage proposal from Dr Joseph Fraenkel. In 1912 she also began an intense relationship with the radical painter Oskar Kokoschka.

Kokoschka was bewitched and obsessed by Alma and their passionate affair lasted for three years. In 1913, he painted an allegorical representation of their love affair, *The Bride of the Wind*—the title of Susanne Keegan's biography of Alma, and the name of Bruce Beresford's film based on the book in 2001. Long after they split, on Alma's seventieth birthday, Kokoschka referred to her as a 'wild creature' and was convinced that they were 'united in the *Bride of the Wind* forever'.

Oskar had tried to persuade Alma to marry him, but Alma's second marriage, in 1915, was to Walter Gropius. Walter and Alma had a beautiful daughter, Manon, in 1916, and travelled between Germany and Austria. Their relationship waned, and in 1918 Alma began an affair with Jewish poet Franz Werfel. She became pregnant to him in early 1918 but their baby son, Martin, died.

Other collections of her songs appeared in 1915 and 1924, including her 1915 setting of Werfel's 'Der Erkennende' and poems by Novalis, Bierbaum and Oehmel. She also published her influential edition of Mahler's letters and the facsimile manuscript of his *Tenth Symphony*. In the same years that Walter Gropius was founding the Bauhaus movement in Weimar, his marriage with Alma was finishing and in 1920 their divorce papers were filed. Franz now was the centre of her life and with

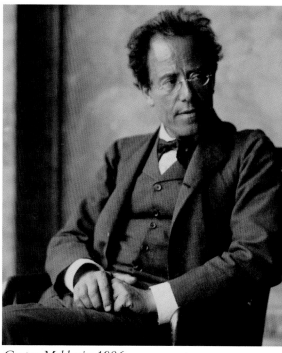

Gustav Mahler in 1906

him, Alma became friends with the composer Alban Berg and his wife Helene. Berg's opera *Wozzek* is dedicated to Alma. At the age of 50, Alma married Werfel, her third husband, in 1929.

Tragedy had not left Alma's side and in 1935, Alma's and Walter's beautiful daughter Manon died from polio in 1935. Alban Berg created a violin concerto 'Dem Andenken eines Engles' (To the Memory of an Angel) in her memory. The Nazi prohibition of Werfel's works forced Alma and Franz to flee Austria and Germany for France. In 1940, they travelled on foot over the Pyrenees mountains to Spain and Portugal, leaving Europe for the United States on board the *Nea Hellas*, the last regular ship from Lisbon.

Alma's constant support for Werfel helped him to achieve his international career, which climaxed in the novels filmed by Hollywood, *The Song of Bernadette* and *Jacobowsky and the Colonel*. When Franz died in Hollywood in 1945, Alma became an American citizen and settled in New York in 1952. She opened her house to artists and writers and wrote her memoirs, published in 1958 titled *And the Bridge is Love*. Alma Schindler-Mahler-Gropius-Werfel died in 1964 and was buried beside her daughter Manon in Grinzing, near Vienna.

'God granted me the privilege of knowing the brilliant works of our time before they left the hands of their creators. And if I was allowed to assist these knights for a while, then my existence is justified and blessed!' she wrote in her memoirs.

Marie Curie

'Marie Curie's greatest discovery was … radioactivity. Pierre Curie's greatest discovery was Marie.' So said one chemist of the famous scientific couple. Marie Curie is known to history as the woman who, along with her husband Pierre, made radioactivity a household word.

MARIE CURIE was the first woman to earn a Nobel Prize—for isolating radium and polonium—and the first person to win two Nobel Prizes. The hardship she endured for her work and her determination to succeed in a male-dominated scientific community has kept her legend alive. Renowned as a pioneering scientist and researcher, Marie Curie was also a woman whose natural compassion compelled her to help others, even if it meant enduring hardship herself. Also part of the Curie folklore is the fact that she died as a result of her exposure to radiation, of leukaemia in 1934. Perhaps less well known are Marie's determination and the resolve that helped her overcome hardship and discrimination throughout her life.

Marya Sklodowska was born in Warsaw, in Russian-occupied Poland, in 1867 to a poor but educated family. Her parents were teachers. Marya learned physics and chemistry from her father and benefited from her parents' regard for scientific knowledge. Her mother died when she was quite young, perhaps forcing Marya to develop the inner strength that served her so well in later life. At 16, Marya graduated from secondary education school, the Russian Lycee in Poland, with a gold medal. She then worked as a governess to help finance her older sister Bronia's studies in France for six years. Once she graduated in medicine, Bronia helped Marya move to France to study as a mature student at the prestigious Sorbonne University.

Marya arrived in Paris in 1891, a 24-year-old who not had any formal education for six years and could not speak fluent French. She changed her name to fit in to the more Francophone Marie and soon distinguished herself as a bright and ambitious student. Despite living in a tiny rented attic where she froze in winter and baked in summer, she devoted herself to her studies. She took her physics degree with honours in mathematics within three years.

Pierre Curie was head of a laboratory at the School of Industrial Physics and Chemistry in Paris, eight years older than Marie and already an established scientist. With his brother Jacques he had discovered piezoelectricity (when pressure is applied to certain crystals, they generate electrical voltage). He was an expert in the field of crystals and magnetic fluctuations due to changes in temperature. Today the temperature at which some materials exhibit a marked change in their magnetic properties is known as the Curie Point, after Pierre and Jacques, and the principle that governs these is known as Curie's Law. He developed a very precise scientific balance, the Curie Balance, which proved vital in Marie's later work.

Marie recognised in Pierre a kindred spirit, saying 'I noticed the grave and gentle expression of his face, as well as a certain abandon in his attitude, suggesting the dreamer absorbed in his reflections.' Pierre 'ardently wooed Marie and made several marriage proposals'. Their intellectual attraction soon strengthened to romantic love and they married in July 1895, in Sceaux, Pierre's home town. They used money received as a wedding present to buy two bicycles, and enjoyed long, occasionally arduous rides together—rare escapes from their demanding schedules.

The pair began a collaboration in their work that would last throughout their careers. Chemist Frederick Soddy said of their relationship: 'Marie Curie's greatest discovery was … radioactivity. Pierre Curie's greatest discovery was Marie.'

Marie embarked on a PhD in physics in 1897 at the Sorbonne and researched x-rays with Henri Becquerel. She became fascinated by the properties of uranium salt, and speculated that there was another, unknown mineral producing the 'uranic rays' that passed through protective shielding to darken photographic plates. Marie concluded that the radiation did not depend on the molecular structure, but was linked to the interior of the atom itself. As a concept this was revolutionary and perhaps her most important contribution to physics.

Marie set to work separating literally tonnes of raw minerals to recover mere specks of the active, but unknown to science elements radium and polonium—named after her native Poland. 'Sometimes I had to spend a whole day stirring a boiling mass with a heavy iron rod nearly as big as myself. I would be broken with fatigue at day's end', she wrote.

It was about this time that she coined the term 'radioactive'. Pierre was so impressed with her research that he abandoned his own field of study—even turning down a Chair at the University of Geneva—and the couple worked together in deplorable conditions until the thesis was complete. Their laboratory was a simple shed, but they shared a passion for their work and enjoyed the privacy. 'One of our pleasures was to enter our workshop at night; then, all around us, we would see the luminous silhouettes of the beakers and capsules that contained our products,' said Marie. The couple refused to file a patent application for their discoveries as they believed all scientists should have free access to their discovery for the pursuit of knowledge.

Marie presented her findings on 25 June 1903 in her doctoral thesis. Members of the examination panel found that Marie's findings represented the 'greatest scientific contribution ever made in a doctoral thesis'. She was the first European woman to earn a PhD in science. The Curies and Becquerel were jointly awarded the Nobel Prize for Physics for their discovery of natural radioactivity. As a team they had established, for the first time, that one element can really be transmuted into another. The discovery of radium revolutionised chemistry and launched the nuclear era.

After winning the Nobel Prize the Curies became celebrities in France and around the world. Pierre took up a post as professor at the Sorbonne in 1904 but he was ill. His legs shook and he was in pain. Both his and Marie's fingers were cracked and they suffered from fatigue—they didn't know about radiation poisoning. Pierre liked to say that radium was a million times more radioactive than uranium and he carried a small vial in his pocket to show friends. Marie kept some

Marie and Pierre Curie in 1902.

radium salt by her bed—it glowed in the dark. Their surviving papers still emit radioactivity.

Tragedy struck in 1906 when Pierre died in a horse-drawn carriage accident in Paris and Marie was left to raise their two young daughters, Irène and Eve. Overcoming social prejudice, she took up her husband's position at the Sorbonne, becoming the first female to teach there.

Despite the high profile of her work, or perhaps because of it, she became the target of spiteful media attention. When she was nominated for election to L'Académie des Sciences, a section of the media launched a campaign of anti-Semitism, sexism and xenophobia to prevent her election. Her exceptional scientific merit notwithstanding, she narrowly lost to an embarrassed colleague, Édouard Branly. The French scientific community was internationally shamed and Marie deeply wounded. Shortly afterwards she was accused of having an affair with a research colleague and, when nominated for the Nobel Prize for Chemistry in 1911, was nearly forced to turn down the honour to avoid humiliating the Nobel Foundation. Marie refused to be cowed; she asserted that the merits of her scientific work should not be obscured by racist, gender-biased slander.

She was awarded her second Nobel Prize, for Chemistry, in 1911. Her influence was crucial to the founding of the Radium Institute (now the Curie Institute) and the Pasteur Institute in Paris in 1914. During World War I Marie, with her daughter Irène, pioneered the use of mobile x-ray vans to find bullets and shrapnel in wounded soldiers.

Marie died of leukaemia caused by her exposure to radiation in July 1934, aged 67, exhausted and almost blind. In 1995, on the orders of President Mitterand, Marie and Pierre's remains were transferred to the Pantheon in Paris. Marie became the first woman buried in the Pantheon.

Marion and Walter in the garden of their Castlecrag home in the 1920s.

Marion Mahony Griffin

The design tender for Australia's capital, Canberra, was won with drawings done by the first woman in the world to be a licenced architect. With Walter Burley Griffin, Marion Mahony Griffin designed and completed over 350 architectural design projects.

MARION LUCY MAHONY was born in Chicago, Illinois, in 1871, the year of the great fire which ravaged the city. Her father was an Irish poet, journalist and educator, her mother a respected teacher and for many years principal of the radical Kaminsky school. Marion's father died when she was 11 and her mother, Clara, brought her up alone. Marion grew up surrounded by a network of strong and influential women, including the suffragette Mary Hawes Wilmarth.

Her cousin, Dwight Perkins, had been to Massachusetts Institute of Technology and graduated as an architect. He encouraged Marion to go there too, and in 1894 she became only the second woman architect to graduate from MIT.

Marion moved back to Chicago after she graduated and took up a position with Dwight. She then met and began working for the internationally-renowned architect Frank Lloyd Wright in 1895, two years after he had started his own studio. Lloyd Wright is recognised as one of the 20th century's greatest architects. Marion's 14 years in Wright's studio would influence her life's work.

Working in his studio, in 1898 Marion became the first woman to take an architectural licence, not just in Illinois, but in the world. Even though she was outnumbered in the male-dominated profession of architecture, Marion forged a unique identity as a dedicated designer.

Frank Lloyd Wright was committed to advancing the ideas and principles of organic architecture, organic education, and conservation of the natural environment. He believed architecture should work in and around its environment and Marion was inspired by his work, having already developed a passion for nature and its relationship with the built environment.

Marion became one of Wright's primary designers and had a close relationship with him and his wife. She was responsible for designing many of the furnishings of his houses, including murals, mosaics, furniture, leaded glass and lighting fixtures, as she was also interested in the personal and intimate nature of domestic architecture.

In a major scandal, Wright sold his practice to Herman Von Holst in 1909 and left his wife and five children in Chicago to live in Germany with the wife of a former client. Marion, described as 'fiery and spectacularly brilliant', completed, and in some cases designed, all his unfinished commissions.

The last house of his which she built was the Adolph Mueller House. She filled the living room's tent ceiling with stained glass and wrapped the home in a continuous pattern of leaded glass. The Mueller houses in Decatur, Illinois, are two of only three Mahony houses remaining in the United States.

Marion recommended that Von Holst hire a young man named Walter Burley Griffin to develop a landscape plan for the Mueller houses. Soon Marion and Walter were working closely together and when Marion married Walter Burley Griffin in 1911, aged 40, it was the beginning of one of the most outstanding artistic collaborations of the twentieth century. Marion became chief draftsman in the Griffin office and her drawing skills breathed life into all of Walter's designs.

In 1911 the Australian Minister for Home Affairs launched a competition to design the nation's capital city. The Griffins' was one of 157 entries. Marion's drawings of Walter's plans were immense. Two and a half metres wide and 9 metres long, they unfolded like Japanese screens. They were so beautiful and impressive that the judges had miniature copies made so as to not be swayed by their presence.

After they were awarded the project, Walter and Marion moved to Melbourne, where they stayed for the next 21 years. Marion managed a private architectural practice, while Walter focused on the planning of the new national capital. Her practice produced designs for some remarkable houses, as well as Newman College at Melbourne University, and the Capitol Theatre.

After a dispute between Griffin and federal government bureaucrats, Griffin resigned from the Canberra project in 1920. In 1924, Marion and Walter moved to Sydney to supervise the development of the suburb of Castlecrag. They designed more than 50 houses, of which 16 were built. Marion and Walter Griffin challenged accepted opinion, and had a vision of a democratic society living compatibly with nature. By 1935, however, they were reduced to designing incinerators in the Sydney area. So Marion, aged 64, and Walter, five years her junior, left Australia to go to Lucknow, India, where their architecture practice was revitalised. Walter died there from peritonitis in 1937 at 60 years old.

Marion returned to America and intended to travel to Australia but the outbreak of World War II stopped her from travelling in the Pacific. She spent the rest of her life writing and designing. She died in Chicago in 1961 at the age of 91.

Her ashes remained in an unmarked grave in Graceland Cemetery before they were re-interred there in 1997. She now rests alongside some of America's greatest architects.

Between the Wars
1920-1939

Lotte Lenya

Lotte Lenya's career ranged from the plays and musicals of her husband Kurt Weill and Bertold Brecht, to Hollywood James Bond films. Her famous portrayal of Jenny and the hit song 'Mack the Knife' brought her to the public gaze as a unique and individual performer.

LOTTE LENYA was born Karoline Wilhelmine Blamauer in 1898, the third child of a cab driver and a laundress in a working class suburb of Vienna. Lenya said 'there was no sign of theatre, nowhere' in her family background, but she was drawn to performance in her early years.

In Zurich in 1914 she studied both classical dance and acting. She gained invaluable experience in opera, ballet and theatre performance under the stage name Lotte Lenja (she later changed it to Lenya). In 1922 in Berlin she auditioned as a dancer for a part in *Zaubernacht*. She was introduced to the composer but could not see him hidden in the piano pit—it was Kurt Weill. She was offered the role but turned it down it out of loyalty to a teacher who had not been offered a one.

In 1924 Lotte was asked by her friend, German expressionist dramatist Georg Kaiser, to collect Kurt Weill from the train station in Berlin. On the journey the pair realised they had met before, albeit briefly, at the audition. It was the beginning of a lifelong collaboration. Two years later, in 1926, they married.

In 1927 Lenya's distinctive soprano voice, once described by a German critic as 'shattered glass', was heard in the first of her many performances in Weill's operas as Jessie in *Mahagonny (Songspiel)*. In 1928 she debuted in what was to become her signature role, Jenny in *The Threepenny Opera,* with its hit, 'Mack the Knife'. In 1929 Weill wrote of Lenya, 'She is a miserable housewife, but a very good actress. She can't read music, but when she sings, people listen as if it were Caruso.'

The rise of Nazism meant Weill and Lenya had no choice but to leave Germany, as both were Jewish. By 1933 their relationship had broken down and they fled to Paris separately. There, Lotte continued her artistic relationship with Weill even though they were divorced. She still performed the role of Anna in the Brecht-Weill opera *The Seven Deadly Sins*. In 1936, still in Paris, Lotte and Weill reignited their relationship and emigrated to New York where they married again in 1937.

Weill adapted easily to life in America as a composer and had some success on Broadway,

Kurt Weill in the 1930s.

especially with *The Lady in the Dark*. Lenya found it more difficult to fit in. She said 'circumstances were difficult for an actress with a German accent in the US in the 1930s and 1940s'.

In 1945 Lotte received bad reviews in her husband's production of *The Firebrand of Florence*, and the show closed after only 43 performances. She never performed again in Weill's lifetime. He suffered a fatal heart attack in April 1950 just after his fiftieth birthday.

It was only after Weill's death that Lotte Lenya was persuaded to return to the stage for a memorial concert tribute to her husband. It was a huge success and revived annually up until 1965. In 1951 she returned to Broadway in *Barefoot in Athens* and married the show's writer, George Davis. Encouraged by Davis, Lenya agreed to revive her role as Jenny in the English version of *The Threepenny Opera*. The off-Broadway production caused a sensation and ran continuously from 1954 to 1961. Jazz and pop recordings of 'Mack the Knife' released locally and internationally, made Lotte Lenya a household name. During their marriage, George Davis had also supported the complex matter of establishing Weill's legacy. When Davis died of a heart attack in 1957, Lenya devoted herself to that job for the rest of her life and set up the Kurt Weill Foundation for music in 1962.

During the 1960s and 1970s Lotte Lenya's voice dropped its distinctive soprano quality and became, as described by a friend, 'an octave below laryngitis'. The solution was to adapt Weill's scores accordingly so she could continue to perform in the Brechtian theatre she was famous for. She also performed successfully in theatre and cinema—as Fraulein Schneider in the original Broadway production of *Cabaret*, and as a procuress in the film *The Roman Spring of Mrs Stone*, for which she was nominated for an Academy Award.

Lotte married twice after the death of George Davis—to painter Russell Detwiler 1962 and briefly to film-maker Richard Siemanowski. Lotte Lenya died in New York from cancer in 1981. She is buried with Kurt Weill at the Mount Repose Cemetery, Haverstraw, New York. Of her time working with Weill and Brecht, Lenya once remarked, 'I was goddamned lucky to get into that gang and survive and make my little contribution'. They were goddamned lucky to have her, too.

Eleanor Roosevelt

Eleanor Roosevelt is one of America's most revered First Ladies. The wife of Franklin Delano Roosevelt, the longest serving president in American history, she tirelessly campaigned for women's rights, minority rights and equality for African Americans.

THE ELDEST OF THREE CHILDREN, Eleanor Roosevelt was born into a wealthy and prominent New York family (her uncle was President Theodore Roosevelt) on 11 October 1884. Her parents—Anna Hall and Elliot Roosevelt—were wealthy socialites. Her mother and one brother died when she was eight, and her father, an alcoholic, when she was 10.

After her mother died, Eleanor and her other brother were raised by her grandmother until she was 15. Eleanor knew she hadn't inherited her mother's good looks, and people called her 'plain and awkward'. But her years at Allenswood boarding school in England helped her to develop into a self-confident and intellectual young woman.

Eleanor liked to party and read good books, and taught dancing to girls in her local neighbourhood. In 1902 at the age of 18 she met Franklin Delano Roosevelt, who also happened to be her fifth cousin once removed, at a party. He was studying at Harvard University and was apparently fascinated by her intelligence and the fact she was opinionated—although she would refer to herself as the 'ugly duckling', She was attracted to his charm and his sense of fun, and people say their relationship was a true and deep romance. They married in 1905 and between 1906 and 1916 Eleanor gave birth to six children, one of whom died shortly after birth.

Like her husband, Eleanor was a Democrat and took a strong interest in politics. In 1910 Franklin ran for the New York State Senate and soon became a popular leader in the New York Democrats. Throughout his political career, Eleanor represented her husband in public life and worked for reforms that they both believed in. It was when she visited St Elizabeth's Hospital in late 1917, during World War I, that she gained huge popularity and respect by using her power as the wife of a well-respected politician to ease a social issue. The navy had taken over buildings at the hospital for injured sailors and Eleanor was horrified by what she saw: 'Poor demented creatures, with apparently very little attention being paid them, gazing from behind bars or

walking up and down on enclosed porches'. She put so much pressure on politicians that Congress increased funds for the hospital, as well as asking the Red Cross for funds.

In 1921, Senator Franklin contracted polio, which made it hard for him to use his legs. Many of their friends and family said that Franklin should retire and stay at home, but Eleanor convinced him to work to restore his health. She travelled to places where Franklin could not go because he was too tired, or because his crutches could not take him there. She played a significant role in his successful political campaigns, making speeches for him and meeting VIPs alongside him. Franklin Roosevelt was elected Governor of New York State and soon after, in 1932, President, as America hit the 'Great Depression'.

For the next 12 years, Eleanor travelled across the country and overseas, visiting places where people needed help, carrying out fact-finding trips for her husband and campaigning for sexual and racial equality. Eleanor would report back to her husband, who was often too sick to travel, about what she had seen and what she thought needed to be

Above: With Franklin in 1933.

Right: Eleanor makes a radio appeal for Red Cross donations in 1940.

done. 'Very early,' she said, 'I became conscious of the fact that there were men and women and children around me who suffered in one way or another.' At a time when it was unfashionable to do so, she spoke out in favour of women's and minority rights, especially for African Americans.

Eleanor wrote a syndicated column called 'My Day' six days a week from 1935 until her death in 1962, in which she expressed her views on the world. She was the first woman to speak before a national political convention and to hold regular press conferences, and she moonlighted as a radio commentator. She fought for what she believed in, and gained worldwide acclaim and respect for being a champion of social justice. Even when President Roosevelt died in 1945, Eleanor's work continued. President Truman appointed her a special delegate to the United Nations, which was meeting for the very first time. She served as a delegate for six years, until she was 68, and headed the group that wrote the Universal Declaration of Human Rights. She was awarded the first ever United Nations Human Rights Prize.

Eleanor Roosevelt was America's best ambassador. 'Send Eleanor Roosevelt' became a famous saying during her lifetime and continues today. She was repeatedly voted America's Most Admired Woman and featured in *Time* magazine as one of the 100 greatest leaders and revolutionaries of the twentieth century.

Alice B Toklas

As the lover, editor, constant companion and household manager of experimental American writer and social commentator Gertrude Stein, Alice B Toklas lived much of her life surrounded by artists and writers. Gertrude wrote her own autobiography in the voice of her companion, in The Autobiography of Alice B Toklas.

ALICE BABETTE TOKLAS was born in 1877 into a middle-class Jewish family, was university-educated and a one-time music scholar. But when she met one of Gertrude Stein's brothers, Michael, in her native San Francisco in 1906, she was keeping house for her family, a situation she didn't enjoy. Michael Stein suggested she go to Paris and see if she liked the European life. So Alice and a friend set off for the Continent, arriving in 1907. They soon met Gertrude Stein in Paris and were welcomed into the circle of writers and painters who gathered around her.

Recalling the moment she met Gertrude, Alice said that 'she was a golden brown presence, burned by the Tuscan sun and with a golden glint in her warm brown hair'. It was, by all accounts, love at first sight. Soon after they met, Alice began helping Gertrude by typing her manuscripts. Around 1910, Alice moved into the house in Montparnasse in Paris with Gertrude and, initially, her brother Leo Stein.

The central belief that united Alice and Gertrude was their shared faith in Gertrude's genius as a writer. The experimental, avant-garde style Gertrude favoured meant that she was not a hugely popular author, but Alice's painstaking editing as well as her emotional support ensured that Gertrude continued writing. Gertrude's writing process involved handwriting (often almost illegibly) her texts into a series of notebooks; when she had finished writing for the day, Alice would type them out, editing and proofreading when necessary. As Gertrude never revised her writing, it is also possible that Alice had much more input into Gertrude's work than we know.

During World War I Gertrude and Alice worked for the American Fund for French Wounded, driving hospital supplies to the front and visiting wounded soldiers. In World War II, they were lucky to escape the concentration camps by sheltering in the French countryside, where the local people referred to them as 'the Americans'.

Alice was an excellent cook and household manager—so much so that some new visitors

Alice B Toklas (right) and Gertrude Stein.

assumed that Alice was the 'hired help', as she always answered the door and the telephone, and oversaw the activities of their servants and kitchen. Gertrude and Alice had pet names for each other that they didn't hide from their friends—Gertrude was 'Baby Woojums', Alice was 'Mama Woojums'. During their life together, their home was visited by a host of well-known literary and artistic figures, such as Pablo Picasso, Henri Matisse, Georges Braque and Ernest Hemingway, and many guests noted that while Gertrude would engage the (usually male) artists in conversation, Alice's role was to entertain the 'wives'—and the two conversations often did not cross over. Alice had keen interests in art herself, producing excellent tapestries, turning designs that Picasso himself would draw for her into tapestried furniture. Hemingway indicated that he thought Alice had a tyrannical hold over Gertrude, but none of the couple's other friends ever mentioned this.

In 1933 Gertrude published her most popular work, *The Autobiography of Alice B Toklas*. It was in fact the story of Gertrude's own life, told as she imagined Alice might have told it. Their friends claimed that Gertrude had captured Alice's conversational style—chatty, observant and easily diverted—perfectly. The book was such a success that Gertrude and Alice embarked on a trip to the United States in 1934, where Gertrude gave a series of well-received lectures.

Late in World War II, Gertrude was diagnosed with stomach cancer. Within months of the diagnosis, in July 1946, she died. Alice suffered greatly, writing days after Gertrude's death that 'the emptiness is so very very great'. A comment in a letter showed her profound sense of loss: 'I wish to God we had gone together, as I always fatuously thought we would—a bomb—a shipwreck— just anything but this'.

Alice lived for another 20 years and busied herself with publishing Gertrude's remaining manuscripts and her own writing. In 1954 she published a book that was to make her an icon and at least as famous as her deeply missed companion: *The Alice B Toklas Cook Book* was a collection of recipes and reminiscences which shed light on her passion for cuisine and on her life with Gertrude Stein. The book contained a recipe (not her own, but offered by a friend) for 'Hashisch Fudge', which contained marijuana. This made the book a cult favourite in the 1960s. Another cookbook, *Aromas and Flavours of Past and Present*, followed in 1958. She lived in France, writing articles for American magazines and newspapers and publishing her autobiography in 1963. Her later years were marked by poverty, as Gertrude's art collection was confiscated by one of the Stein heirs.

Alice converted to Catholicism, asking her priest if this would allow her to see Gertrude when she died. She wrote, just a few years before her death, 'It was Gertrude Stein who held my complete attention, as she did for all the many years I knew her until her death, and all these empty ones since then'. Alice died in 1967 and was buried beside Gertrude in the Cimetière du Père Lachaise, Paris.

War, Peace and Freedom
1949–1959

Frida Kahlo

Artist Frida Kahlo met Mexican muralist Diego Rivera when she was a high school student and grew into an artist whose work is recognisable all over the world, particularly her self-portraits.

MAGDALENA CARMEN FRIDA KAHLO Y CALDERÓN was born on 6 July 1907. She was the third of four daughters born to Guillermo Kahlo, a photographer and painter who had emigrated to Mexico from Germany, and his wife Matilde Calderón y Gonzalez, a Mexican of Spanish and indigenous descent. Recognising his daughter's intelligence at a young age, Frida became her father's favourite, and he taught her about art, photography, literature, archaeology and natural science. She was the only child in the family to attend secondary school, entering the elite National Preparatory School in 1922, where she was one of only 35 girls out of 2000 students. It was here, at 16, that she met her future husband Diego Rivera for the first time. He was the most famous artist in Mexico and was painting a mural in the school auditorium—she was a high-spirited teenager, trying to get his attention with practical jokes.

Frida planned to study medicine and with this in mind studied subjects such as biology, zoology and anatomy. Her life took an abrupt turn when 1925 the bus she and her boyfriend were on collided with a trolley car. She was found amongst the wreckage skewered by one of the metal handrails which had entered through her pelvis and exited through her uterus. The accident destroyed her chance of ever bringing a pregnancy to full term. Suffering broken bones, including her back in three places, she spent one month in hospital and another three confined to bed. While bedridden, Frida began to paint with her parents' encouragement. They arranged for a special easel to be made and attached a mirror to the bed's canopy so she could use herself as a model.

Frida also developed a passion for politics and joined the Communist Party, where she again met Diego Rivera. He was twice her age, three times her size and a well-known philanderer but she surprised her friends and family by falling in love with him and against all advice married him in 1929. Her mother disapproved of the union and famously described it as 'an elephant marrying a dove'. Diego helped Frida, encouraging her distinctive primitive style of painting and her technical proficiency. 'Frida Kahlo is the greatest Mexican painter,' he said. Her work is destined to be multiplied by reproductions and will speak, thanks to books, to the whole world.'

Frida and Diego at The Blue House.

In 1930 the couple went to America where Rivera thrived. But Frida was unhappy and her homesickness was exacerbated by her second miscarriage and the death of her mother. In 1933, Rivera became involved in a scandal over his inclusion of comrade Vladimir Lenin in a mural for the Rockefeller Centre. Frida insisted they return to Mexico where they moved into a house with two studios attached by a footbridge, the famous Blue House.

Diego was depressed about his departure from America and in 1934 had an affair with Frida's sister Cristina, forcing the couple to separate. They were reconciled later that year but both continued to have affairs throughout the rest of their married lives—Frida most famously with Leon Trotsky, who had been granted political asylum in Mexico.

In 1938 Frida began to sell her paintings for the first time. 'This way I am going to be able to be free, I'll be able to travel and do what I want without asking Diego for money,' she said. With the encouragement of French writer and surrealist Andre Breton, Frida travelled to New York alone for her first solo exhibition. She went to Paris and had another solo show in 1939. She was recognised as a great talent by Pablo Picasso, who claimed she was his artistic equal. The Louvre bought one of her self-portraits, *The Frame*, their first artwork by a 20th century Mexican artist. When she returned to Mexico, she was not met by her husband's congratulations but another of his affairs. By 1939, they were divorced.

Frida was devastated by the divorce and plagued by chronic pain, depression and illness, which had always been worsened by Diego's philandering. 'I suffered two grave accidents in my life,' Frida once said. 'One in which a streetcar knocked me down ... The other accident is Diego.'

She began painting some of her most distinctive works—*The Two Fridas* (1939) and *Self-Portrait with Cropped Hair* (1940). She also exhibited alongside Diego at the International Exhibition of Surrealism in Mexico City. In late 1940, encouraged by a mutual friend, Frida and Rivera remarried in California and returned to Mexico. Frida had operations on her back and her foot, and her right leg was amputated below the knee in 1953. Rivera cared for her during her increasing periods convalescence. In 1953, Frida was given a solo exhibition in Mexico City's National Institute of Fine Arts Contemporary Art Gallery. Still recovering from the surgery on her right leg, she was taxied to the exhibition in an ambulance and held court from a bed in the gallery.

When Frida Kahlo died in 1954, weary from years of illness, Diego dedicated The Blue House to the Mexican people in her honour.

Simone de Beauvoir

Simone de Beauvoir achieved fame not only as a philosopher, author and feminist but also for her 'open relationship' with Jean-Paul Sartre. Her book, The Second Sex, *heralded the writings of future feminists, most notably Germaine Greer's* Female Eunuch.

SIMONE-ERNESTINE-LUCIE-MARIE BERTRAND DE BEAUVOIR was born on 9 January 1908, the elder of two daughters in a typically *petit bourgeois* Parisian family. Her father, Georges Bertrand de Beauvoir, was an agnostic lawyer fallen on hard times, and her mother Françoise (née) Brasseur was a convent-educated Catholic girl with a large dowry, which the family subsequently lost in World War I. Simone's father encouraged his daughter's intellect throughout her childhood, but would have preferred she married well rather than pursue the successful career she enjoyed.

Simone passed her school exams (the *Baccalaureate*) in mathematics and philosophy and went on to study philosophy at the Sorbonne. At 21 she became the youngest person ever to pass the philosophy *aggrégation* exam, in which she came a close second to Jean-Paul Sartre. Sartre, then 24, asked to meet 'le Castor' (the Beaver), the nickname given to her by her then boyfriend René Maheu that would stick to her for life. Simone became one of Sartre's elite circle, and what he lacked in physical style, he made up for intellectually.

Simone and Sartre became famous as a couple—yet they led independent lives, living in separate hotel rooms and never marrying or having children. They sat at separate tables in the cafés of St Germain de Pres to write and see friends, but remained committed to each other as their 'essential' love. De Beauvoir explained in her book *The Prime of Life*: 'One single aim fired us, the urge to embrace all experience and to bear witness concerning it.'

De Beauvoir had many love affairs, as did Sartre. Her bisexuality meant they even shared lovers. They famously made a pact to share every detail of each other's dalliances, and many of Simone's were retold in her novels, *She Came to Stay* (1943) and *The Mandarins* (1954).

In 1940 the Nazis occupied Paris. De Beauvoir was teaching in Rouen but was fired from her academic post in 1941 by the Nazi government. Sartre had been drafted into the French army and was imprisoned by the Germans until April 1941. Both returned to Paris in 1941 politicised

Simone de Beauvoir and Jean Paul Sartre in Paris in 1946.

by their experiences, and became involved in an underground group of writers called Socialism and Liberty. When that group dissolved both wrote novels of 'active resistance'. Simone de Beauvoir's *The Blood of Others* (1943) has been described as one of the most important novels of the French Resistance.

After Paris was liberated in 1944 and the war had ended, de Beauvoir joined Sartre and others in founding and editing the most prominent political and philosophical journal of its day, *Les Temps Modernes*. She published much of her work within its pages and remained one of its editors until she died.

Sartre and Beauvoir became famous for their contributions to the philosophical movement 'existentialism'. In his 1946 lecture 'Existentialism is a Humanism', Sartre explained the key to the movement as 'existence preceding essence'.

De Beauvoir developed these ideas in *The Second Sex*, arguing that 'one is not born a woman; one becomes one' through social conditioning and the choices we make in our lives. In 1949 de Beauvoir's public identity dramatically split from Sartre's when *The Second Sex* was published. Women,

Simone de Beauvoir wearing a brooch designed by artist Alexander Calder.

she wrote, had historically been treated as the 'other', an aberration of the 'normal' male sex. The book sparked a revolution amongst the French middle class women which eventually spread to America and beyond. Sadly Sartre thought 'women's rights were a bit of a joke' and did not encourage or support his partner's seminal work. In the end, de Beauvoir's contribution to the evolution of feminism proved to be much more widespread than any political movement Sartre put his passions into.

Simone de Beauvoir had opportunities to relinquish herself of her lifelong pact with Sartre but did not take them up. Other serious loves in her life included the American novelist Nelson Algren, who wanted to marry her, and Claude Lanzmann, a Paris-based film-maker with whom she lived from 1952 to 1959. She wrote about these relationships openly, much to the shock and annoyance of Algren who wrote savage reviews of her books in retaliation. She could never be completely loyal to any other man than Sartre.

Simone de Beauvoir lived in an apartment overlooking Sartre's grave and when she finally died of pneumonia, was buried alongside him in the Cimetière du Montparnasse in Paris.

Eva Perón

Millions still mourn her, many still hate her, but the whole world knows her name. Evita lived a short life in front of microphones, cameras and crowds. The personality cult she built around herself and her husband, Juan Perón, help him hold Argentina's presidency for a decade. After her death her followers campaigned for her canonisation as a saint.

Born María Eva Duarte in regional Los Toldos, Argentina, in 1919, Evita's early life was difficult due to the early death of her father. (Her parents were unmarried, and later Evita changed her birth certificate to conceal this fact—and to make herself appear three years younger.) With four children to feed and clothe, times were hard for Evita's mother Juana Duarte, who worked as a seamstress. Evita was desperate to escape, and in 1935 made her way to Buenos Aires to become an actress. She had some success with touring comedy shows, but it was in radio that she made her name, securing a weekly show of her own.

In January 1944, Evita and a fellow actress talked their way into a benefit concert for victims of an earthquake in San Juan and she found herself sitting beside Colonel Juan Perón. The previous year, Perón had been part of a military coalition that overthrew Argentina's government and he was now a member of the new government.

There are many versions of what they said to each other—in Evita's she tells Juan, 'If your cause is the people's, then I will be at your side, no matter what I have to sacrifice for it'. In his later years, Juan bluntly recalled her 'red' hands and 'thick' ankles and claimed, 'I was not attracted by her looks. It was her kindness'.

Rumour has it that soon afterwards Evita ejected Juan's mistress from his home and moved in with the leader 25 years her senior. He didn't object. She quickly gained enormous influence over Perón, which stunned and dismayed his colleagues. By all accounts, their union was not sexually passionate, but they looked after each other. Evita was unfailingly loyal, using her radio show to extol the virtues of her would-be president. In October 1945, Juan was thrown out of the government and exiled. But his popularity was so great that workers in Buenos Aires rebelled and he was reinstated just days later. Within a week, Juan and Evita married.

It was during Perón's presidential campaign for the national elections in 1946 that Evita came into her own. Juan called her 'my shadow'—she accompanied him everywhere, listening, learning and making great rhetoric-filled speeches to stir up the working classes. It was unusual for a woman to do this, and the middle and upper classes of Argentinian society were vehemently opposed to her position. But when Juan became president in 1946, Evita was able to greatly influence Argentina's public policy. She set up a new charitable foundation and used the contributions from business, unions and the national lotteries to fund new hospitals, schools and orphanages. She also formed the Perónista Feminist Party in 1949 and was responsible for the law reform that finally gave Argentinian women the right to vote. She supported the unions, travelled internationally with Juan (looking consistently glamourous), and knew how to manipulate his affairs so that anyone she suspected of betraying either of them could be removed.

Juan would tell her not to work so hard, perhaps so she could be more 'wifely'. But there is no doubt in anyone's mind that without Evita's public presence, and the devotion of her beloved working classes—the *descamisados*, or 'shirtless ones', as she called them—Perón would not have enjoyed the personal success and position that he did.

Evita's early death (she was only 33) left her followers with a lasting image of their heroine. In 1950 she fell ill, but still managed to gain the nomination for the vice-presidency in the 1951 elections. She had cancer—first cervical, then uterine—and her death would be slow and intensely painful.

She soon renounced her candidacy for vice-president in a radio speech, under pressure from military leaders, but maintained her famously rhetorical (and not altogether modest) tone: 'On the day when they write a marvellous chapter of Perón's life, they will say the following about me: next to Perón, there was a woman who was devoted to communicate the hopes of the people to him. Of this woman, we only know that the people lovingly called her Evita.'

But her cancer was progressing, and despite surgery she continued to decline. Her doctors concealed her condition from her, but were shocked to discover, just before she died, that she had known about it all the time.

On 4 June 1952, Evita made her final public appearance when Perón was elected for his second term as president—with a frame attached to the inside of her dress to keep her almost skeletal frame upright. (She had insisted on this, telling her doctor, 'I will not stay in this bed, unless I am dead.') After that day, she barely left her room again.

She died on 26 July 1952. For 13 days, thousands of mourners flocked to see her body, embalmed and placed in a closed glass casket. It was an unprecedented display of grief, and her

Eva and Juan Perón in Buenos Aires, Argentina, in the 1940s.

death made headlines around the world. Soon her followers began campaigning for her to be canonised as a saint.

After her death, the Perónist regime lost its energy, and Juan was overthrown in 1955. Over the next 20 years, Evita's remains were stolen, hidden and moved several times, but finally interred with those of her family. She became more famous after her death, and when the musical *Evita* was first performed in 1978 she was once again making news.

Since then, a movie of *Evita,* starring Madonna, has only increased the mythical quality of this determined woman's life. She used to call her husband the Sun, and he called her his shadow—but the brilliance of Evita's continuing fame has demonstrated just the opposite.

Lee Krasner and Jackson Pollock in the studio at 'The Springs', East Hampton, in 1953.

Lee Krasner

Lee Krasner's marriage to one of the most influential artists of the 20th century dominated her life and her public profile. After Jackson Pollock's death in 1956 and subsequent exhibitions of her work, Lee was finally recognised as an important artist—not only because of her effect on Pollock's career, but for the originality and integrity of her own vision.

LIKE THOUSANDS OF OTHER EUROPEAN JEWS escaping poverty and discrimination, Lee Krasner's father, Joseph, left the Ukraine for America in 1905. When he found work he sent money back for his wife and family to join him. Lena Krassner (she later changed the spelling) was born in 1908 in the East New York section of Brooklyn. Her mother Anna was said to be 'contentious, pragmatic, and grim faced'—perhaps because she had married at 11 and had given birth to five children before she was 20.

Lee grew up in a traditional Jewish household, where women were supposed to be modest and support their fathers and husbands. But from an early age, she rebelled against her family, and refused to conform to their expectations. Against all her parents' values, Lee wanted a career in the arts. In 1922 she graduated from Brooklyn Primary School and applied to Manhattan's Washington Irving High School, the only one that permitted girls to major in art. Her application was rejected and she spent a dismal year in a pre-law program at a girls' high school in Brooklyn, supporting herself by decorating lampshades, china and felt hats. She applied again to Washington Irving High and was accepted.

Lee's years at Washington Irving only served to toughen her up against poor grades and teachers' ridicule of some of her work. She graduated and applied to the Women's Art School of The Cooper Union for the Advancement of Science and Art and was accepted. Desperate to get away from everything she had grown up with, she began a new life in Manhattan.

Manhattan before World War II was packed with Jewish immigrants from all over Western and Eastern Europe. It was a melting pot of ideas and practice, in a city and country undergoing huge change. Lee went to the National Academy of Design in New York, from 1928-33 to further her ambition of becoming an artist. But the rigid discipline of copying plaster casts proved too repressive. She wanted to be challenged.

In 1938, she began studying with Hans Hofmann, who encouraged students to be daring and to work in their own way. Hofmann had been a student with Henri Matisse in Paris and was determined to bring that thinking to New York. He was suave, enthusiastic, a great teacher, and a showman. It is said that between 1933 and 1958 Hans Hofmann left an indelible mark on an entire generation of American artists—including Lee.

Lee was sociable and determined, and threw herself into the world of artists around her, particularly the group of young, mostly New York painters who became known as Abstract Expressionists. They worked in a variety of styles, but generally shared a commitment to creating large-scale, abstract works, an interest in Jungian psychological theories, and a belief that expressiveness was achieved through the physical process of painting. She had some intense relationships, which failed, and was said by many to be looking for someone, a soul mate to hook up with.

In 1941, John Graham was arranging a show of French and American painters and asked Lee for a large painting. Lee was flattered. Graham showed her the list of other abstract expressionists, which included someone she had not heard of before, Jackson Pollock. The son of a farmer from Cody, Wyoming, the 'moody cowboy' lived around the corner from her, and she decided to see what he was like.

She went to his studio and knocked on the door. For once, Pollock answered—he usually ignored it. Her own rendition says that she was 'bowled over' by the sight of his paintings and fell in love with his work and not him. This interpretation is disputed by many, who said she had seen him often before and had picked him out of the crowd as a marriage possibility. Some of her friends said she came away from their first encounter madly in love with his remoteness and scowling masculinity. Others say that none of his work at this stage could have been said to bowl anyone over, that it came nowhere near the later intensity he would discover. Whatever the reality, that meeting was the beginning of a historical relationship that would cloud her own identity as an artist until his death.

'American and French Paintings' opened in 1942 in New York, a milestone in Lee's career. Her paintings and Jackson's hung alongside those of Henri Matisse and the great cubist Braque. By this time the pair were 'meshed', or as one commentator described, 'psychologically embedded in each other'.

The 1940s saw outstanding visual experimentation in New York and Lee Krasner was in the middle of it all. She was one of the few women to play a major part in the transition from modernist painting in the 1930s to abstract expressionism in the 1950s.

From that point, Lee became obsessed with Jackson's career and put her own work on the backburner. She showed him off to the people she had met at Hofmann's school, took him to as many artists' studios as she could, and introduced him to critic Clement Greenberg. She sublimated herself into his work and his career. Greenberg says in Steven Naifeh's *Jackson Pollock: An American Saga*: 'Pollock couldn't do anything for himself. If he went to the station to buy himself a ticket, he'd get drunk along the way. Lee had to remind him to eat.'

Lee in 1953 in East Hampton.

Lee spent the next 20 years trying to steer Pollock's extraordinary talent and vision 'away from alcohol and onto the canvas'. Her first victory was to link him up with the only person buying contemporary art, Peggy Guggenheim. With Lee's determination to push him towards artistic success, and her talent for publicity and promotion, Pollock's career took off.

Managing his career was easier than managing his personal problems. Pollock had been drinking from an early age and was never in control of it. He was a notorious binge drinker, with lapses into depression and self-destruction. Pollock responded strongly to nature and Lee hoped that out of the city his focus would change. She moved them into a house in East Hampton where she painted in a converted bedroom upstairs while Pollock painted in the barn—where he created his famous 'drip' paintings.

In 1945 Lee insisted they married. But while Pollock's prices were soaring on the art market, he was drowning in alcoholism. Binge drinking and reckless driving, depression, violence and evasion made him a difficult partner. When he started an affair with Ruth Kligman under their own roof, Lee knew it was all coming to an end. In 1956 she decided to go on a trip to Europe, and pleaded with Jackson to come with her. But he never travelled outside the United States and Lee left alone. It was the last time she would see him. Speeding in his convertible, he wrapped himself, Ruth and her friend around a tree and was killed.

For months Lee felt unable to work. Her mother died not long after Pollock, and Lee said later that she could hardly handle colour in that darkness. Eventually, she moved back to the New Hampton house and painted in Jackson's studio.

She lived for another 20 years, during which she produced the biggest, boldest works of her career. Shows in America and London strengthened her position as an artist. Her widowhood was comfortable, from an economic point of view. Prices for Pollock's works rose even more after his death, enough to ensure Lee's livelihood and to establish the Pollock-Krasner Foundation after her own death.

She died in 1984, aged 75.

Sirimavo Bandaranaike

The world's first female prime minister, Sri Lanka's Sirimavo Bandaranaike, was thrust into the pages of history after the assassination of her husband in 1956.

S IRIMAVO RATWATTE was born in 1916 into the aristocracy of Sri Lanka (then Ceylon). Her father was a former Senator and her mother a well-known physician. A bright student, she was educated by Roman Catholic nuns at St Bridget's school in the capital, Colombo.

In 1940, aged 24, Sirimavo met and married a lawyer and politician 17 years her senior, Solomon West Ridgeway Dias Bandaranaike. Some said that in her he had at last found his intellectual equal. Sirimavo was not afraid to challenge him and enjoyed the social life of his career.

As Solomon rose through the government to hold a cabinet and senior ministerial position, Sirimavo gave birth to their three children and supported him as a politician's wife. In 1948 the fortunes of Ceylon began to change. As the country finally gained independence from Great Britain, Solomon became deeply embroiled in the rush for power. In 1951 Solomon formed what became the Sri Lanka Freedom Party and with Sirimavo converted from Christianity to Buddhism, which appealed to the nationalists. In 1956, Solomon's socialist coalition seized power in the elections and he became Prime Minister. But Solomon's coalition of parties was unable to solve the country's economic problems or the dispute over which language should be the official one. His government was hampered by infighting among Sinhalese and Tamils and lacked direction.

Sirimavo's life was turned upside down in 1959. On 25 September, as her husband was in the capital Colombo, a dissident Buddhist monk took aim and shot him dead. Sirimavo found herself widowed with three children. Reflecting on that moment in a parliamentary debate 20 years later, she said: 'It was a historic moment for the country and a decisive moment for me. My dilemma was whether to devote the entirety of my time and effort to look after my three orphaned children or to sacrifice the personal interests of my family for the principles for the country and for the party for which my husband gave his life. Acting according to conscience, I chose the latter and accepted the leadership of the party to serve within the limits of my capacity the masses of this country—it was not for love of office that I yielded to the appeals of my party.'

Sirimavo Bandaranaike campaigns in the 1960s.

In 1960, Sirimavo was asked to lead the party which her husband had founded. Some called her the weeping widow as she frequently burst into tears during the election campaign while vowing to continue her late husband's socialist policies. When Sirimavo led the Sri Lanka Freedom Party to a resounding victory in that election, she became the world's first female prime minister. Many said said her success was due to the people's love and respect for her late husband. But her introduction into political office was by no means smooth. This was a country still in turmoil and struggling with its identity. Within a year of her election victory she had to declare a state of emergency after a civil disobedience campaign by the country's minority Tamils. They were outraged by her decision to drop English as the official language and her order to conduct all government business in the language of the majority Sinhalese population.

The state takeover of foreign businesses upset the Americans and the British, who imposed an aid embargo on the country. Bandaranaike moved her country closer to China and the Soviet Union and argued for non-alignment. At home, she crushed an attempted military coup in 1963, and one year later, she was defeated on a confidence vote, losing the general election that followed.

Politics was now in her blood, and six years later Sirimavo was back with a big majority in the 1970 elections. Her second term saw a new Constitution, which finally broke all links with Britain. In 1972 her party turned the Dominion of Ceylon into the Republic of Sri Lanka.

The Indian prime ministers Jawaharlal Nehru and Indira Gandhi, had very close family connections with the Bandaranaike family and as a result Indo-Sri Lanka relations during her rule were unique. When a left-wing uprising almost toppled her government and Sri Lanka's small ceremonial army could not deal with the insurgenc, Sirimavo was saved by her skilful foreign policy. The country's non-aligned friends rushed to her help. In a rare move, both India and Pakistan sent troops to Colombo and the rebellion was crushed.

WT Jayasinghe's book about the boundary talks between India and Sri Lanka offers a glimpse into the powerful women's world in which Sirimavo moved. When the talks between the officials of the two sides were locked in stalemate, Jayasinghe recounts: 'I suggested to Bandaranaike that she seek a one-to-one discussion with Indira Gandhi, as the entire negotiations were in jeopardy…' The Indian prime minister met with Bandaranaike and Jayasinghe 'in the rear verandah' of her residence. 'I remember Indira Gandhi telling Mrs Bandaranaike, almost complaining, that neither of her sons was interested in politics…'

By 1976, Bandaranaike was more respected abroad than at home. Her great triumph that year was to become chairman of the Non-Aligned Movement and host the largest ever heads of state conference the country had ever seen. At home, unemployment, inflation, food shortages and ethnic tensions continued to escalate and even the nationalisation of tea and rubber in 1975 did not help the economy. Sirimavo suffered a crushing election defeat in 1977 and was then expelled from parliament for abuse of power in 1980 and banned from public office for seven years.

The 1980s were her dark days—a political outcast rejected by the people who had once worshipped her. She spent the next 17 years in opposition warding off challenges to her leadership of the Freedom Party, even from her own children.

Always the politician, she played her ambitious daughter Chandrika and son Anura against each other, holding onto control despite losing every subsequent general election. She met her match in Chandrika, who outmanoeuvred her mother to become President of Sri Lanka in 1994, when a Freedom Party-led coalition won power in the general elections. Chandrika appointed her mother prime minister, a post she held until she resigned because of ill health in 2000.

The 2000 general election saw Chandrika survive an attack by a suspected Tamil Tiger suicide bomber on the final day of campaigning. On Sirimavo's way home from voting in that election, she suffered a heart attack and died aged 84. Chandrika was re-elected for a second successive term as Sri Lanka's president.

Joanne Woodward

Joanne Woodward is not only an esteemed stage, film and television actress, she is also celebrated as the woman who has been married to actor Paul Newman for almost 50 years. Their marriage is a rare example of a successful, long-lasting Hollywood relationship.

ACTING WAS ALWAYS IN JOANNE WOODWARD'S BLOOD. She was born in Thomasville, Georgia, in 1930. At the age of nine, when the movie *Gone With the Wind* premiered in 1939, she convinced her mother to drive her to see it in nearby Atlanta. When she finished high school—where her acting skills had already been noticed—she spent two years at Louisiana State University until her father's job moved the family to New York. Here Joanne took the opportunity to begin acting classes at the Actors Studio, and later at the Neighbourhood Playhouse Drama School. After some success in theatrical productions, she scored her first film role in *Count Three and Pray* in 1953.

For the young actress, 1953 was a landmark year in more ways than one. While she was understudying a role in the Broadway play *Picnic*, Joanne met Paul Newman, one of its principal actors. He was already married, with three children, but that didn't stop them falling in love. According to Joanne, it was Paul's sense of humour that made all the difference. They didn't marry at once, and in the years before their marriage Joanne's star continued to rise. She debuted on Broadway in 1954, and won the Best Actress Academy Award for her performance in the 1957 film *The Three Faces of Eve*, in which she played a woman with three distinct personalities. After Paul's difficult divorce finally came through, Joanne and Paul married in Las Vegas in 1958.

This began many years of the couple working together on films—either acting opposite each other, or with Paul wearing the director's hat and Joanne taking a lead role. These included *The Long Hot Summer, Paris Blues, A New Kind of Love* and *Mr and Mrs Bridge*. By the mid-1960s, they had three daughters— Elinor ('Nell'), Melissa and Claire ('Clea')—and Paul's celebrity was beginning to reach fever pitch after the release of *The Hustler* in 1961.

Joanne later said that these were difficult years for her: 'When I was young and had young children, it was terrible. I hated it. When photographers would shove me aside to get to Paul, when women would try to tear his clothes off, when I was trying to protect the children.' She has also

Joanne Woodward celebrates her Oscar with Paul Newman at The Beverly Hilton Hotel in 1958. She won Best Actress in The Three Faces of Eve.

admitted to a little professional jealousy in those years. But their relationship endured, and is regarded as an inspirational one, considering the pressures it has faced and the constant attention it drew in its earlier, more fragile days.

Unlike other actresses who find their careers dimming as they reach middle age, Joanne has continued to appear in films, plays and television series throughout her life. During the 1960s and 1970s she completed many films, and her more recent screen appearances include the Academy Award-winning *Philadelphia* in 1993. As recently as 2005 she was nominated for an Emmy Award for her performance in the television series *Empire Falls*.

Over her career, in addition to her Academy Award, she has won Golden Globe Awards, several Emmy Awards, a Cannes Film Festival Award, a New York Film Critics Circle Award and a BAFTA—and been nominated for countless others.

And there's no sign that Paul has ever been anything but enormously supportive of her career. She and Paul have also worked together for political issues, campaigning for the US Democratic Party. They regard themselves as environmentalists, and Paul's food empire—'Newman's Own'—is a global business with over US$150 million a year in turnover, from which all profits go to charity. Joanne also campaigns for many causes, including research into Alzheimer's disease.

These days, Joanne Woodward is just as famous as her husband, and there is rarely an interview with Paul in which Joanne and their marriage is not mentioned. When they are asked how they managed to keep it together, they have given a variety of serious and flippant answers.

Joanne has often commented that Paul always charmed her with his sense of humour: 'Sexiness wears thin after a while and beauty fades, but to be married to a man who makes you laugh every day—ah, now that's a real treat'. She's also indicated that having a man who'll cook for you is a guaranteed winner. Paul has commented on the 'sizzle' in their relationship, both on and off the screen, and has joked that Joanne must be putting something in his food. Whatever the reasons, both of themthe two have been able to continue fruitful professional careers, both together and separately.

Joanne and Paul live in the small town of Westport, Connecticut, and in 2000 its rundown theatre, the Westport Country Playhouse, was revitalised when Joanne took an interest in it. She is now Artistic Director of the theatre, and even convinced Paul to come back to the stage and appear in a production there. So it seems that after years of marriage and of carving out a lively, energetic existence together, they are not interested in slowing down.

For this Hollywood-born relationship, coming out the other side of the more challenging times has been all about making a promise to work things out: 'We just made a commitment to one another to stay together.' It looks like they've kept their promise.

Lucille Ball

The 'First Lady of Television' was a film and television actor and comedian. She and first husband, Desi Arnaz, created I Love Lucy, *one of the most popular sitcoms of all time. Lucy was also the first female head of a television studio.*

Lucille Desiree Ball was born in Jamestown, New York, in 1911. Lucy and her brother were raised by their grandparents and working mother after their father died when Lucy was three. Grandfather Fred loved the theatre, and family outings often included local vaudeville shows. Lucy was encouraged to create her own plays and participate in school drama.

At 15, Lucy dropped out of high school to pursue an acting career. She applied to the John Murray Anderson School for the Dramatic Arts in New York but was told at auditions that she was 'too shy' and spent the rest of her teens working in casual jobs. In 1930 she had some success as a fashion model and won minor roles performing on Broadway under the name 'Diane Belmont'. When Hollywood noticed her as the Chesterfield cigarettes girl in 1933 she began to have some success as a performer, this time in films. With small movie roles in top pictures and leads in lesser B Grade films, Lucy earned the title among Hollywood circles as 'Queen of the Bs', although she acted with Bob Hope, Katharine Hepburn and Ginger Rogers. Despite appearing in over 60 films during the 1930s and 1940s, it seemed Lucy would never be a star.

In 1940, Lucy met Cuban-born musician Desiderio (Desi) Arnaz while filming the musical *Too Many Girls*. Desi was famous for bringing the conga line to American audiences, for his recordings and as bandleader of his own orchestra. Despite cultural differences and a difference in age (he was six years her junior), the pair fell in love and eloped later that same year.

Their different work schedules and commitments meant the newlyweds were frequently apart. Lucy soon discovered his infidelities and filed for divorce, but they made up and agreed to stay together. By the late 1940s, in a bid to save their relationship, Lucy and Desi agreed to work together on a project. In 1950 the CBS television network approached Lucy after the success of a CBS-produced radio sitcom *My Favorite Husband*. Lucy had co-written and starred in the series as a scatterbrained housewife. CBS asked her to turn the idea into a television format. She refused

Lucille Ball in a 1949 still from Jacques Tourneur's film, Easy Living.

A 1955 studio portrait of Lucy and Desi.

unless they accepted Desi as co-star.

The network resisted the idea of a 'mixed marriage', and it was only after Lucy and Desi toured the idea as a successful vaudeville act and filmed the pilot episode of *I Love Lucy* at their own expense that CBS picked it up. The show was a hit and would remain the most popular sitcom on television from 1951 to 1957. Onscreen, the couple played struggling musician Ricky Ricardo and his wife Lucy Ricardo, a housewife with showbusiness aspirations known for her crazy schemes. The role gave Lucy plenty of scope to explore her comic acting. Desi became the show's executive producer and together they founded Desilu Studios.

In 1951, Lucy gave birth to the couple's first child, Lucie. In 1953, in a television first, the pregnancy and birth of their son, Desi Jnr, was written into *I Love Lucy*. The live-to-air episode where 'Little Ricky' was born attracted an audience across America. *I Love Lucy* won more than 200 awards, including five Emmys. It pioneered filming techniques and the concept of the 'rerun'.

By the late 1950s Desi's womanising had not stopped and he developed an alcohol problem. In an attempt to relieve the pressures of producing a weekly sitcom, they finished the show after 179 episodes and taped a new format, *The Lucy-Desi Comedy Hour*. Their hour-long specials continued for three more years until the marriage collapsed, with Lucy filing for divorce the day after filming finished, in March 1960.

The following year, Lucy married Gary Morton, a stand-up comic 13 years her junior. When she returned to weekly television with *The Lucy Show* in 1962, she bought out Desi's share of Desilu, making her the first woman to become head of a television studio. Desi's drinking got worse and he gave up showbusiness, but Lucy developed Desilu into one of the biggest production companies in the world, selling to Paramount in 1967 for $17 million.

Lucy appeared in the Broadway musical *Wildcat* in 1961 and later in several acclaimed films, including *Yours, Mine and Ours* (1968) and *Mame* (1974). *The Lucy Show* ran for six years and *Here's Lucy* ran on prime time television in 1974. Lucy's last public appearance was at the 1989 Academy Awards. Exactly one month later she died.

The Sexual Revolution
1960-1979

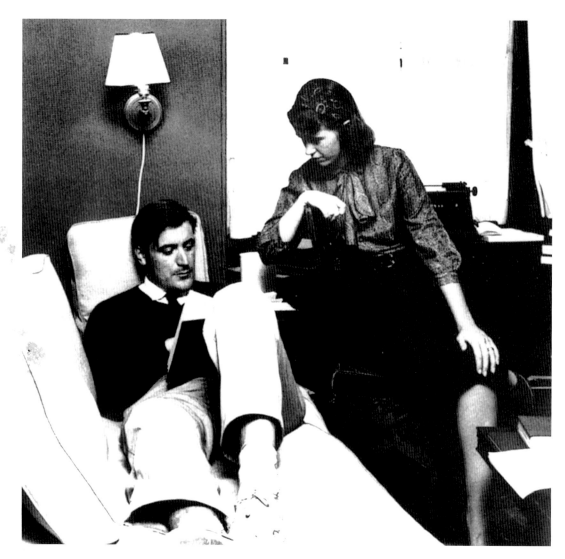

Sylvia Plath and Ted Hughes in Boston in 1958.

Sylvia Plath

During her lifetime, writer Sylvia Plath achieved less commercial success than her husband and poet Ted Hughes. After her suicide in 1963, Sylvia's work was published for a new audience, bringing her fame and a cult following that remains undiminished today.

SYLVIA PLATH, BORN IN 1932 IN JAMAICA PLAIN, Massachusetts, was writing poems and stories almost as soon as she could read them. Her first piece of writing was published when she was eight years old, and she sold her first poem—to *Seventeen* magazine—when she was still in junior college. She was motivated, popular and academically-gifted and when she finished high school she won a scholarship to study at Smith College in Massachusetts. In her four years at Smith, Sylvia also suffered a serious breakdown in 1953 and attempted suicide. She was admitted to a psychiatric hospital and underwent a course of electric shock treatment.

Sylvia recovered to finish her degree at Smith and her poetry was accepted for publication in *Harper's* and *The Atlantic Monthly*. She was awarded a Fulbright scholarship to study literature at Cambridge University and it was here she met Ted Hughes in early 1956, at a party celebrating the literary journal he had just published with friends. Sylvia had read his poetry, been excited by it, and gone to the party with the intention of introducing herself to him and his fellow poets. In her journal she wrote an account of their meeting, which Ted later indicated was wildly overdramatised. According to Sylvia, Ted was 'that big, dark, hunky boy, the only one there huge enough for me'. In a secluded room at the raucous party, 'he kissed me bang smash on the mouth and ripped my hair band off …and my favourite silver earrings: hah, I shall keep, he barked. And when he kissed my neck I bit him long and hard on the cheek, and when we came out of the room, blood was running down his face'.

They became involved in an all-consuming love; as Sylvia wrote in her journal, 'Daily I am full of poems; my joy whirls in tongues of words … I do not merely idolize, I see right into the core of him … I have never been so exultant'. They married in June 1956, initially keeping the marriage secret in case Sylvia's scholarship was withdrawn. Ted was as besotted with Sylvia's vibrancy and her talent as she was with him. It was at Sylvia's insistence that Ted submitted a book of poems, *The Hawk in the Rain*, in a contest in 1957. He won, and the collection was published to acclaim. They moved to Massachusetts, where Sylvia began teaching at Smith College and Ted's fame grew. But Sylvia found teaching difficult and could not achieve the uncompromisingly high standards she had set for herself. She began seeing a therapist again, writing that 'I have a good self, that loves skies, hills, ideas, tasty meals, bright colors. My demon would murder this self'. Part of her 'demon' was also the nagging fear that Ted might be unfaithful to her.

When the couple returned to England in 1960 their first child, Frieda, was born. Sylvia was happy. Her first collection of poetry, *The Colossus and Other Poems*, was published in England, and while its reviews were good it did not make the splash that Sylvia may have hoped. Ted's star continued to rise as his poetry, plays and children's stories were publicly praised.

In 1961, the family moved to Devon in the south of England. As a new mother, and with Ted working in London much of the time, Sylvia felt isolated. Their son Nicholas was born in 1962, and while it is clear that Sylvia adored her children, her poems and journals from this time reveal her desperate unhappiness coupled with dramatic, euphoric upswings. She was not achieving the success she had hoped from her writing: *The Colossus* was finally published in America, but to a lukewarm reception; her semi-autobiographical novel, *The Bell Jar*, was also accepted by an English publisher, but Sylvia chose to have it published under a pseudonym.

In mid-1962, Sylvia discovered that Ted was having an affair, and in a rage she burned stacks of his writing, and possibly the draft of a sequel to *The Bell Jar*. After two tense months, Sylvia and Ted separated. Sylvia, Frieda and Nicholas moved back to London. Her stability declined and she was again in the care of a psychiatrist and trying new medication while at the same time writing some of the best poetry of her life. But on 11 February 1963, Sylvia's 'demon' finally claimed her. After opening her children's bedroom window, sealing the cracks in their door with towels and leaving them some bread and milk, Sylvia turned on the gas oven in the kitchen and laid her head inside. She was found dead the next morning. The children were discovered cold but safe.

Ted had the grim task of identifying Sylvia's body. It seems beyond dispute that he destroyed poems, altered others and removed parts of Sylvia's journal. But when he arranged for the publication of the brilliant, passionate *Ariel* poems Sylvia wrote in the last years of her life, he helped give Sylvia the widespread acclaim that she had not found in her lifetime. Another publication of *The Bell Jar*—this time under her real name—in the mid-1960s, followed several collections of poetry plus journals and letters.

Ted has been portrayed as a philandering monster, a suffering husband and everything in between. While Ted tried to redress the balance in his 1998 collection *Birthday Letters*, it is the image of Sylvia's isolation and tragic death that endures.

Elizabeth Taylor

Dame Elizabeth Taylor—actress, philanthropist and veteran of eight marriages—has outshone every one of her famous and not-so-famous husbands with her beauty, talent and extravagant behaviour.

OUT OF ALL HER HUSBANDS, Elizabeth Taylor has said she was happiest with producer Mike Todd and Richard Burton, her most famous beau, who she married twice. Theirs was one of the best-known celebrity relationships of the 1960s and 1970s, and it formed the passionate centrepiece of a life that has weathered over 60 years of relentless publicity.

Born in 1932 in London, Elizabeth Rosemond Taylor moved with her family to the United States just before World War II, and was soon 'discovered' by a talent scout, making her film debut in 1942, aged 10. *Lassie Come Home* (1943) and *National Velvet* (1944) launched her as a child star. Elizabeth made an easy transition into 'grown-up' film roles. During the 1950s she became one of the most famous and respected female actors in film, starring in movies such as *Giant* (with Rock Hudson), *Raintree County* and *Cat on a Hot Tin Roof*. The new decade began spectacularly with a 1960 Academy Award for her performance in *Butterfield 8*.

Elizabeth's relationships with men were gaining her even more media attention. As she said in a 1997 interview, 'I really love men ... I'm more of a man's woman. With men, there's a kind of twinkle that comes out. I sashay up to a man'. She married her first husband, Nicky Hilton (Paris Hilton's great-uncle), in 1950 when still a teenager. The actor Michael Wilding became her second husband in 1952, and the couple had two sons. Next was film producer Mike Todd who died in a plane crash only a year after their marriage, leaving Elizabeth with a new daughter. But it was during her next marriage—to Eddie Fisher—that she met Welsh actor Richard Burton.

According to her friends, Elizabeth could never abide passive or submissive men for long. Until Richard Burton entered her life, only Mike Todd had come close to the kind of strength she seemed to prefer. Elizabeth and Richard first met briefly in the 1950s; after their first meeting, Elizabeth reputedly said of Richard that he was 'rather full of himself', while Richard thought she was 'the Mona Lisa type, beautiful but very sombre'. Their affair began on a film set in Rome in 1962, when they were cast in the epic *Cleopatra*. Both were already married, but their very public

affair began almost as soon as rehearsals did. Observers commented that they did seem to be in love, despite the tempestuous nature of their relationship. As Elizabeth said in her memoir, 'Richard Burton was surely my fate.' The film studio tried to dump her from *Cleopatra*, but Elizabeth apparently refused, saying, 'Nobody tells me who to love or not to love.'

During their tumultuous relationship—which included marriage in 1964, divorce in 1974,

Richard Burton and Elizabeth Taylor in California in 1970.

remarriage the following year and divorce again in 1976—Elizabeth and Richard made six more films together, and it was for her performance in *Who's Afraid of Virginia Woolf* opposite Richard in 1966 that she won her second Academy Award. But their relationship included wild drinking sprees and—at least for Elizabeth—an increasing dependence on prescription drugs. Richard was still womanising, the media was still scrutinising their behaviour, and the relationship disintegrated.

After her second divorce from Richard, Elizabeth remarried quickly, to politician John Warner in 1976. Her weight became a talking point. In a 1977 interview, Elizabeth agreed: 'I am fat. God, yeah. I can hardly get into any of my clothes, but I eat out of enjoyment'.

After divorcing John Warner in 1982, Elizabeth and Richard Burton were reunited in the play *Private Lives*. The reviews were scathing, and there was plenty of gossip about Elizabeth's frequent absences due to 'illness'. She and Richard maintained a cool distance. After the play's closure, Elizabeth admitted herself to the Betty Ford Centre. She recovered and relapsed, then wound up in the clinic again in 1988—where she met her final husband, Larry Fortensky. They married in 1991 and divorced in 1996.

It was the death from AIDS of her long-time friend Rock Hudson in 1985 that motivated Elizabeth to raise awareness of the disease. In 1985 Elizabeth helped establish the American Foundation for AIDS Research and was its first national chairman. In 1991 she founded the Elizabeth Taylor AIDS Foundation. Since then, Elizabeth has continued to work for the AIDS cause, despite her poor health. When she was awarded the title Dame of the British Empire in 1999, Elizabeth responded, 'Well, I've always been a broad, now it's a great honour to be a dame!'

Madame Mao

Jiang Qing was the fourth wife of China's Mao Zedong. From humble beginnings she led the Cultural Revolution to become the most powerful woman in China. After Mao's death her downfall was swift.

JIANG QING WAS BORN LI SHUMENG in the Chinese province of Shantung in 1914. Her mother was one of her father's concubines and their relationship was not a happy one. In 1929 Shumeng joined a theatrical group and moved to Shanghai where she worked as an actress and became known as Lan Ping. She joined the Communist Party in 1933, but left Shanghai when the Japanese nationalist forces invaded China in 1937. She settled in Yunan, the centre of the Chinese Communist resistance.

The young actress was required to attend 'Party School' to study Communist ideology and history. It was here she first encountered Mao Zedong when he gave a speech at the school. In 1939 Lan Ping used her contacts to transfer to an arts college. Mao visited to give another speech, and afterwards was interested enough to seek her out . She was 24; he was 45. They began an affair which was frowned upon by Party officials—Mao was still married to the respected Communist He Zizhen. Mao appreciated Lan Ping's strong will and observed that it could work well for his own career, even if she was not too knowledgable about politics.

Lan Ping was eager to move up in the world and find an outlet for her abundant energy. 'Sex is engaging in the first rounds,' she said, 'but what sustains interest in the long run is power'. When Party officials tried to block the relationship, Mao reportedly told them, 'Without Lan Ping's love, I can't go on with the revolution.' Mao was soon able to divorce He Zizhen and marry Lan Ping who was already pregnant with his child. They also decided she needed a new name for her role as the great leader's wife; they chose Jiang Qing, meaning 'green waters'. It was agreed that Jiang would not be permitted to take any role in politics—she was to be first and foremost a wife. She was furious at this limitation, but agreed and soon gave birth to the couple's daughter, Li Min.

As the years passed, Jiang grew in confidence and began to exert more influence on affairs outside her domain. In 1949, Mao achieved his political objectives—the Chinese revolution was successful, and the Communist Party had control of China. Jiang, however, was physically ill, and over the next ten years she spent considerable time being treated for cervical cancer, liver disease and respiratory illnesses.

By now the romance with Mao was over, and he resumed having affairs with young women. Jiang was determined to hold on to the marriage and was forced to reconcile herself to his wandering sexual appetite. The 1960s were to be Jiang's 'golden era', and she became as well-known as her husband. Mao had by this time been relegated to one-third of a ruling party, and was now convinced that the only way to move ahead was to purge the Party of anything which was not 'revolutionary'—including his two co-leaders. Jiang Qing took on the task of 'reforming' the arts. All operas and plays were to have stories which illuminated the class struggle.

This was the beginning of the infamous Cultural Revolution, which stymied education, stifled China's economy, caused widespread famine and killed or imprisoned scores of Mao's 'enemies' for more than ten years. Jiang Qing's role in manipulating Chinese culture was profound: she had operas and theatrical productions rewritten, insisted that dancers and orchestras performed only sanctioned 'revolutionary' material, and tracked down almost every person who had ever done her wrong and had them arrested and imprisoned. In 1969 she became a member of the Communist Party Politburo.

By the 1970s, Mao's health was failing. Jiang Qing gathered together a loyal 'Gang of Four' who gained political influence and hoped to rule after Mao's death. Mao knew Jiang was ambitious to become an 'Empress', but he did not seriously try to stop her.

In his final weeks of Mao's life in 1976, he became sentimental about their relationship, but Jiang appeared more nervous than grief-stricken—she knew much of her power in the eyes of the people stemmed from Mao's approval of her. He died in September 1976, and the Gang of Four soon proposed Jiang as Chairman of the Communist Party. Public opinion had, however, turned against her. A rival faction staged a dramatic coup and arrested Jiang and her supporters.

Jiang was imprisoned for the next four years, but at her well-publicised trial in 1980 she was defiant, confessing to none of the charges against her, and abusing the court and her enemies whenever possible. Replying to the accusations that she had acted against Mao's wishes, she declared, 'What I did followed Mao's line and the Party's line. What you are doing now is asking a widow to pay her husband's debt. To you all, I say I am happy and honoured to pay Chairman Mao's debt'. The 'trial', however, was never intended to set her free, and she was again denounced for her role in the Cultural Revolution and imprisoned—in gaol, in hospital or under house arrest—for the rest of her life. Jiang fell victim to throat cancer, but refused to have any treatment. She began her memoirs but tore them up.

In May 1991, after several suicide attempts, she made a noose and hanged herself. She was 77.

Jacqueline Kennedy-Onassis

*Jacqueline Kennedy was an enigmatic, iconic and stylish First Lady.
When President John F Kennedy was assassinated by her side in
1963, she retreated into widowhood. But fame wasn't finished with her
when she reinvented herself as the rich and successful 'Jackie O'.*

JACQUELINE BOUVIER was born into wealth. Though her parents divorced when she was quite young, she grew up surrounded by privilege. Her father was a stockbroker. She grew up in the Hamptons area of New York and received an upper-class education at institutions including Miss Porter's School in Connecticut (a senior high school that doubled as a finishing school for 'refining' young ladies), Vassy College in New York, the Sorbonne in Paris and, finally, George Washington University, Washington, where she completed a bachelor's degree.

At a dinner party in 1952, she met a handsome young Democratic Party congressman, John Kennedy. Jackie rarely discussed her relationship with the media, although she did once say that she and John had a 'very spasmodic courtship, conducted mainly at long distance with a great clanking of coins in dozens of phone booths'. After becoming a senator in 1953, he proposed to her over the phone while she was in London working as a photographer and reporter. In September 1953 they were married.

When John won the 1960 presidential election, Jackie quickly established herself in the White House as a patron of culture, taste and style. She redecorated the White House with early nineteenth-century furnishings and art. For the first time in over 60 years, she brought babies into the White House. After an early miscarriage and a tragic stillbirth, Jackie had two children—Caroline and John Junior. Something else the Kennedys were famous for were the stories of John's infidelities, which were reputedly prolific. He was linked with high-profile actresses such as Marilyn Monroe and Kim Novak. Jackie, again, was tight-lipped, and never alluded to their private

relationship in interviews, although she is recorded as once declaring, 'I don't think there are any men who are faithful to their wives'.

In 1963, came the unthinkable tragedy. Just four months after she lost another baby—Patrick, who lived for only 39 hours—John F Kennedy was assassinated in an open motorcade as she sat beside him. It was an event that America, and much of the world, will never forget. She faced television audiences all over the country wearing the bloodstained clothes that she'd refused to change—she wanted the people to see the horror. Later, she refused to take sleeping pills, fearing they'd affect her ability to play a central role in organising John's funeral.

Jackie and Aristotle Onassis leave an Athens nightclub in 1969 after her fortieth birthday.

After the events of 1963, Jackie became private, protecting her children from media attention and consistently refusing to discuss the assassination. This was a pact she kept with herself until her death 30 years later. She was essentially out of the public eye for five years after John's death.

But in 1968 she reappeared in an almost scandalous fashion. In June, John's brother, Robert, was assassinated, and again America mourned. A few months later, Jackie married wealthy Greek shipping magnate Aristotle Onassis, shocking her family and sending the media scurrying for 'scoops'. He was 28 years her senior, and they had a somewhat unromantic pre-nuptial agreement stipulating property rights and financial matters. Aristotle fuelled speculation about the oddities of the relationship by saying that 'Jackie is a little bird that needs its freedom as well as its security and she gets them both from me ... And I, of course, will do exactly as I please. I never question her and she never questions me.' Jackie, of course, was largely silent on her marriage.

When Aristotle died in 1975, Jackie received just over US $20 million from the settlement and moved back to New York, starting a career in book publishing. She soon became a senior editor with Doubleday. For for almost 20 years she worked and made a name for herself as a perceptive editor who was adept at dealing with her authors.

Even when she was diagnosed with non-Hodgkin's lymphoma—a cancer that affects the lymphatic system—in January 1994, she continued working through her chemotherapy. But, unable to break the cancer's hold, she died in May, with her companion of seven years, businessman Maurice Tempelsman, at her side. She was buried, as she had requested, beside John in Arlington National Cemetery.

Yoko Ono

Yoko Ono, has always been a prolific musician and avant-garde artist. Vilified for her supposed role in the break-up of The Beatles, Yoko was already high-profile in artistic circles when she met John Lennon. The experimental composer, film-maker, conceptual artist and ambassador for peace has never shied away from her own confronting vision.

YOKO ONO WAS BORN IN 1933, the eldest of three children, to a wealthy aristocratic family in Tokyo. Her father, Eisuke Ono, who was a frustrated pianist turned banker, discouraged Yoko's musical aspirations. Her mother, Isoko Isuda, was from one of Japan's wealthiest banking families. Yoko has often described her relationship with both parents as cold and distant. While her mother entertained society's elite, Yoko and her siblings were raised by nannies and tutors. The family moved for a time to California when Yoko was a toddler, but went back to Japan in the lead-up to World War II, where they survived the bombings of Tokyo in 1945.

Returning to the United States in the early 1950s, the family settled in Scarsdale, New York. Yoko studied music at Sarah Lawrence College and became involved with a bohemian scene of artists, poets and musicians. Despite her parents' disapproval, she married a fellow student and composer, Toshi Ichiyanagi, in 1956 and moved to Manhattan, into the avant-garde scene of New York's Greenwich Village.

Theirs was an 'on again, off again' relationship. The couple experienced financial difficulties and separated in 1961 when Toshi returned to Japan to pursue his career. Yoko followed in 1962. Despite never having met Yoko, jazz musician and film producer Anthony Cox tracked her down in Tokyo after hearing about her from friends in New York. Toshi filed for divorce after a period in which the three lived together in Tokyo, with Yoko and Anthony involved in a relationship.

Cox managed and financed Yoko's work in the early 1960s, by which time Yoko was part of the art movement known as Fluxus. Yoko gave birth to Kyoko, in 1963, but it was Cox who managed the domestic and financial front while Yoko pursued her artistic ambitions. Despite a certain status among her peers, however, Yoko's work was for the most part derided or ignored in the mainstream until a film called *Bottoms* (1966) achieved notoriety. The film—literally a film of

Yoko and John in New York in 1980.

close-ups of hundreds of naked bottoms—earned Yoko an invitation to work in the UK. Yoko met John Lennon at an exhibition of her work at the Indica gallery in London in November 1966. John appreciated the humour and wit of her work and the two began a friendship that eventually led to an affair. Their relationship became public in 1968. After the inevitable breakdown of their marriages, and the awarding of custody of Kyoko to Yoko, Yoko married John in March 1969. Their Amsterdam honeymoon at the Hilton Hotel became famous as their first 'bed-in', in which John and Yoko received the press for seven days in their pyjamas, promoting world peace.

John and Yoko created the Plastic Ono Band in 1969—an identity used to describe works by Lennon and Ono and whoever happened to be performing with them. They used the name until 1975 for both solo and joint efforts. By the end of 1969 both John Lennon and Paul McCartney had effectively left The Beatles.

During the early 1970s Yoko was intensely creative, politically active and had to deal with her role as Mrs John Lennon. Added to this was the tragic scene when Anthony Cox kidnapped

Kyoko in 1971 and vowed John would never have custody of his child. He had become a Christian fundamentalist, and initiated his daughter into a Doomsday cult known as The Walk. He brainwashed Kyoko into thinking her mother was evil. For three decades, moving from continent to continent, Kyoko evaded investigators paid by Yoko to find her. Contact was only established when Kyoko, now married to a devout Christian in the United States, herself became a mother and approached Yoko in 1998.

John was constantly threatened with expulsion from the United States for his outspoken opposition to the Vietnam War. Yoko was demonised in the media as 'causing' the Beatles' break-up, while John was berated for leaving his former wife Cynthia and their son Julian. The inherent racism of the media attack on Yoko, combined with the heroin drug abuse they had been engaged in since the late 1960s, led to their relationship collapsing under pressure.

After a 15-month separation, the couple reunited in 1974 and their son Sean was born in 1975 in New York. The late 1970s is sometimes referred to as their 'silent period', with John focusing on raising Sean at home while Yoko began to manage the Lennon businesses. Neither recorded during this time. She enjoyed time with her son and husband, managed Lenono Music which controls the couple's songs post-1973 (Lennon's music prior to this is controlled by Sony), and continued the search for her daughter. In 1980, their collaborative album *Double Fantasy* was released. This revival was to be tragically short-lived: in December 1980 John was murdered outside their apartments The Dakota. Yoko was walking ahead of John when he was shot by deranged fan Mark David Chapman.

Devastated by John's death, Yoko emerged to become musically active throughout the 1980s, recording and releasing albums, with some underground, though little commercial, success. Her album *Starpeace* (1985) was a concept album promoting world peace in the Cold War era.

In 1992, *Onobox*—a compilation of six CDs of Yoko's work—was released. A comeback was declared in 1995 with the release of *Rising*, a collaboration with son Sean. During the 1990s she gave two concert tours and composed two off-Broadway musicals. In recent years, cutting-edge DJs have begun remixing her songs for dance music, giving them a contemporary edge. Yoko's music proved to be highly influential, particularly among post punk 'new wave' bands such as Talking Heads and The B-52s.

Still causing controversy as an artist even as she approaches her mid-seventies, Yoko also continues to exhibit new artwork. In 2002, she inaugurated her own peace award for artists in 'regions of conflict'. Yoko Ono lives in New York City where she continues to keep her husband's work and memory alive while exhibiting, recording and performing. Her productivity, experimentation and diversity as an artist have earned her an increasingly respectful following.

Linda McCartney

Lady Linda came into the glare of publicity when she married Beatle Paul McCartney in 1969, ending the dreams and ambitions of millions of girls. Her life cut tragically short by cancer at 55, Linda left behind a unique identity that fused social commitment, animal rights activism and creativity as a photographer and musician.

LINDA EASTMAN was born in 1941 in New York. Her father was a successful lawyer and she was educated at the prestigious Scarsdale High School, then majored in fine art at the University of Arizona. While Linda was at university, her mother was killed in a plane crash. Linda was so badly affected that she sought comfort in marriage to a man named Melvin, a geophysics student. Shortly after she gave birth to Heather. But the marriage didn't last and they divorced soon after.

Linda returned to New York and worked for *Town and Country* magazine in the early 1960s as a photographer. Taking up an opportunity to photograph the Rolling Stones on a yacht on the Hudson River, Linda started down a path that enabled her to unite her two passions—music and photography—and she began to photograph musicians, including Jimi Hendrix, the Doors, the Who, Simon and Garfunkel, Bob Dylan, Otis Redding and the Beatles. And she found a ready market for her work. Linda continued to take photographs throughout her life, exhibiting in some 50 galleries worldwide, from South America to Australia, and working for *Rolling Stone* magazine.

It was when Linda was photographing groups for *Rock and Other Four Letter Words* in 1967 that she met Paul McCartney. The pair fell in love and Paul broke up with his girlfriend at the time, actress Jane Asher. The British press were devastated that Paul was dating an American divorcee and single mother and not their English rose. It was the beginning for Linda of a lifetime of battling with the media's perception of her.

Paul and Linda were married on 12 March 1969. The media also looked for scapegoats when the Beatles broke up in 1970, and Linda and Yoko Ono were both accused of somehow helping cause the split. Paul and Linda's marriage endured and they had three children in the 1970s— Mary named after Paul's mother, then Stella and James, named after Paul's father.

Linda McCartney with one of her photographs.

Linda began studying piano and Paul was keen that she become part of his new band, Wings, so they wouldn't be apart. She joined as keyboard and vocal performer and went on a record-breaking world concert tour with the band in 1980, playing over 100 shows in 13 countries.

Wings won several Grammy Awards, and became one of the most successful bands of the 1970s. Linda developed her musical talent by writing and recording her own music. She released over ten singles over 23 years from 1973, including *Mister Sandman* and *Sugartime*.

In 1997 Linda gained the official title of 'Lady' when her husband became another in the long line of pop stars given knighthoods by the Queen of England. A vegetarian and ardent animal-lover Linda was a vocal advocate for animal rights. 'I won't eat anything with a face' is one of her well-known quotes. She worked extensively for the Council for the Protection of Rural England and Friends of the Earth, to highlight environmental dangers.

In 1989, she published her own guide to vegetarian cookery, *Linda McCartney's Home Cooking*. The book has become the biggest-selling vegetarian cookbook ever in the United Kingdom and a bestseller in the United States, with more than 250 000 copies sold.

In 1991 Linda launched her own range of ready-made vegetarian meals in the UK: a massive success, with some five million meals consumed by September 1991. Linda McCartney's vegetarian food range has been so successful in the UK that her meals are now on the menu at London's famous Hard Rock Café.

Her family was always important to her. Both Linda and Paul supported their children's creativity and have always included Heather in their family. Heather is a potter. Their daughter Mary McCartney has followed in Linda's footsteps and is a professional photographer and animal rights campaigner. Mary took the last moving photographs of her mother. Stella McCartney was appointed chief designer at the French couture house Chloe in March 1997 and from there has developed her own collection. James McCartney is a musician and sculptor.

In 1995 Linda was diagnosed with breast cancer which eventually spread to her liver. Her relationship with Paul had always been good—they were rumoured to not spend more than a week apart—but it was during this time, that her suffering drew them closer than ever. It has been rumoured that, at one time, Paul even shaved off his hair when the chemotherapy caused Linda to lose hers in a bid to share her experience.

On 17 April 1998 Linda died at their ranch in Santa Barbara, California with Paul at her bedside. She was 56. A collection of solo recordings, *Wide Prairie*, was issued posthumously that same year. Paul made a moving tribute to Linda in two songs on his latest album *Flaming Pie*. He penned 'Calico Skies' and 'My Love for Linda' while she was undergoing treatment for breast cancer. Paul began a new life when he married Heather Mills, but the relationship folded in 2006.

Linda on the job as photographer at the press launch of the Beatles album Sergeant Pepper's Lonely Hearts Club Band *in 1967.*

'Calico Skies'

'It was written that I would love you
From the moment I opened my eyes
And the morning when I first saw you
Gave me life under calico skies
I will hold you for as long as you like
I'll hold you for the rest of my life.'

Cleo Laine

*'Queen of Jazz' Cleo Laine married jazz composer and musician
Johnny Dankworth and became a member of his band. From there she
won widespread fame both as a singer and an actress.*

CLEMENTINA CAMPBELL was born in 1927 in London and from an early age showed talent as a musician. Her parents, Jamaican-born Alec Campbell and her English mother Minnie Hitchin, encouraged their daughter's interest in performing, sending her to dance and vocal classes. Clementina especially admired Judy Garland and was later influenced by jazz greats Ella Fitzgerald and Billie Holiday.

She left school at 14. Her parents had separated and Cleo's mother—unwilling to accept money from Alec—could not afford to support her at school. She left school for a hairdressing apprenticeship (which she never finished) and auditioned for singing roles. However, the disruption caused by World War II and an early ill-fated marriage meant that it wasn't until her mid-twenties that she was able to seriously pursue her singing.

Cleo's first husband was George Langridge, eight years her senior. She met him through friends during WWII when he was enlisted in the navy. They married when Cleo was 17, in 1944, and after the war George returned to his job as a tiler. Their son Stuart was born in 1945. The couple struggled financially and had little in common; although he was content, Cleo grew increasingly frustrated as a wife and mother and longed to pursue her musical ambitions. In 1951 she auditioned for a place with leading jazz group, the Johnny Dankworth Seven.

Her incredible voice, its power and range, caught Johnny Dankworth's attention and his band offered her the job as singer—legend has it that Cleo bargained Johnny up from his offer of six pounds a week to seven. Clementina was now Cleo, and during the 1950s she made several recordings with the band. Johnny began writing music to test and showcase her impressive vocal range. Cleo's marriage to George Langridge eventually broke up in 1954. Cleo had fallen in love with Johnny and owing to her touring schedule, Cleo's mother and sister were awarded custody of her son Stuart.

By 1958 Cleo was ready to break out on her own. 'It was when I decided to be on my own, that he asked me to marry him. He thought he was getting a cheap singer, but what he got was an expensive wife!' They married that same year. While John's band went on to become a major jazz orchestra, Cleo turned to her other interest, acting.

Cleo's first theatrical role saw her performing at London's Royal Court Theatre in 1958, in *Flesh to a Tiger*. Her performances included roles in plays by Euripides, Shakespeare and Ibsen, as well as stage musicals. Her singing repertoire was expanding to include pop, soul and classical.

Considered by Cleo as the couple's masterpiece, the album *Shakespeare: And All That Jazz* was released in 1964. She received a huge reception during a tour to Australia in 1972 which alerted the couple to the possibilities of a wider audience. Her debut at New York's Carnegie Hall in 1973 was a popular and critical sensation. Tours of North America followed, along with a succession of record albums and television appearances. Since then, the pair have continued to tour the world with sell-out shows.

Three concert albums made at Carnegie Hall over a ten year period were a success, with the 1983 album *Cleo at Carnegie: The 10th Anniversary Concert* winning Cleo a Grammy award for Best Female Jazz Vocalist, the first such award for a Briton. She recorded with flautist James Galway, guitarist John Williams and singer Ray Charles. Her live concerts continued at venues such as London's Royal Albert Hall, and performances with symphony orchestras throughout the world, with some broadcast on television.

Her career in musical theatre, which had earned her acclaim in London's West End productions of *Showboat* and *Collette*, continued in America with star roles in *A Little Night Music* and *The Merry Widow*. Cleo's appearance in the Broadway hit musical *The Mystery of Edwin Drood* earned her a Tony nomination and Theatre World Award. Other musical credits include *Seven Deadly Sins* and *Into the Woods*.

Cleo was made an Officer of the Order of the British Empire (OBE) in 1979 for her services to music. In 1997 she became Dame Cleo Laine. True to her versatility, she is the only singer to earn Grammy nominations in the female jazz, popular and classical categories. She holds honorary doctorates from several universities and awards from the British Jazz Society and the British and US recording industries, among others.

Cleo and Johnny (now Sir John Dankworth) also raised two children, a son and daughter, both of whom as adults have gone on to become jazz musicians. Now approaching 80 and still touring internationally, the couple live in Buckinghamshire in the UK. Their joint and solo performing and recording careers continue, along with their work for charities, including The Wavendon Allmusic Plan, founded in 1969 to educate people about music.

Johnny these days gets second billing—it is Cleo Laine who heads the act.

Tina Turner

Tina Turner overcame incredible hardships to triumph as one of the world's most commercially successful female rock artists, with record sales of over 60 million. Her marriage to Ike Turner was notoriously violent, and ended in divorce. Tina went on to sell more concert tickets than any other female performer in history and won seven Grammy awards.

ANNA MAE BULLOCK was born in 1939 to a sharecropping family in Nutbush, Tennessee. Her ancestors were African American, Navajo and Cherokee. Her parents separated when Anna and her older sister were young, leaving their daughters in the care of their grandmother. From an early age, Anna enjoyed singing and dancing to the sound of the radio or the church organ. In 1956, when their grandmother died, 17-year-old Anna moved with her sister to St Louis to be with their mother. St Louis nightlife was an exciting contrast to the rural poverty of the girls' hometown. Though still at high school, Anna found work singing in music venues.

The Kings of Rhythm were a popular local R&B band led by guitarist Ike Turner, eight years Anna's senior. One night, Anna was called up to sing on-stage with the Kings. Ike was impressed, not only by her singing but also by her innate talent as a performer. Her ambitions to become a nurse were forgotten as she was brought in to cover for a male singer who failed to show up for a recording session for the single 'Fool in Love' in 1959.

Ike's intention was to remove the vocals later, but when he heard her version of the song, he changed his mind. They became involved shortly after the success of this single, although Ike's 'involvement' included having over 100 other girlfriends during their marriage. Ike changed Anna's name to Tina Turner even though they were not yet married. Cynics would say that both the name change and the marriage were a way of Ike linking himself to her potential stardom, and the subsequent fame and financial success he craved. 'Fool in Love' became a hit, and the group was renamed The Ike and Tina Turner Revue. With one son already to another musician from the band, Tina married Ike in Mexico in 1960 and gave birth to a second son. Tina raised her two boys along with Ike's two sons from his previous marriage.

During the early 1960s, Tina's raw energy made the Revue a solid touring act. By the late 1960s, however, Ike worried that superstardom was eluding him. Irrational from drug abuse, he began to blame Tina for the Revue's lack of number one hits. Ike's erratic, controlling and violent behaviour towards his family and others started to earn him an ugly reputation. After years of living in fear of her husband's intimidation, womanising and drug addiction, Tina attempted suicide in 1968.

> *Collaborations with David Bowie, Eric Clapton and Mick Jagger*
> *among others ensured her status as one of rock and roll's greatest stars.*

It was her introduction to Buddhism in 1975 that gave Tina the strength she needed to escape the abusive relationship. Later, when asked why it took her so long to walk away from Ike she replied, 'I didn't know anything else—or anybody else. And I wanted to sing.' She finally left Ike—and the band—in 1976. Fearing reprisal and wanting to be completely free of her husband, she did not pursue a settlement but famously left the marriage with nothing but 36 cents and a gas station credit card, as well as the debts accrued when months of bookings were cancelled.

Several solo albums recorded during the late 1970s, as Tina approached 40, were not well-received, and she struggled for years on the lounge circuit, seemingly vindicating those who believed the singer could not make it without Ike's musical input. By the early 1980s, however, with the help of new management, a number of hit singles in Europe and the UK earned her a deal with Capitol Records. Her solo album *Private Dancer* scored several hits. Her comeback was rewarded with four trophies at the 1985 Grammy Awards.

In that same year she starred in the film *Mad Max III: Beyond Thunderdome* which also spawned a number two hit with its theme tune. Collaborations with David Bowie, Eric Clapton and Mick Jagger among others ensured her status as one of rock and roll's greatest stars. World tours and album releases continued into the 1990s. Her autobiography *I, Tina* became a best-seller and was the basis of the 1993 film *What's Love Got to Do With It*. Announcing her retirement from the concert stage in 2000, Tina continues to record and play live at smaller venues. In 2004, at the age of sixty-five, she released a career retrospective entitled *All The Best*.

Tina's varied achievements and iconic status means she enjoys a huge fan-base worldwide. Her longstanding popularity in Europe saw Tina settle permanently there in 1986 with her German-born partner, Erwin Bach. Ike Turner, meanwhile, never quite recovered from the loss of Tina.

His drug and financial problems grew during the 1980s. Though since 'clean' and remarried, in 1991 he was in prison for drug-related offences when he and his ex-wife were inducted into the Rock and Roll Hall of Fame.

Cher

From a teenage offsider of Sonny Bono in Sonny and Cher, to solo singing star, acclaimed actor and celebrity, Cher has lived many lives. She acknowledges it was her partnership with Salvatore 'Sonny' Bono that set her on the path to stardom. But it has been her own persistence and abilities that have formed the megastar we know today.

CHERILYN SARKISIAN WAS BORN IN 1946. Her father was Armenian, and although her mother married and divorced him three times, the young Cherilyn had little to do with him. She struggled at school due to dyslexia (which she didn't discover until she was 30), and in her teenage years was something of a tearaway as her family, including stepfathers and half-sisters, moved around between California and New York. When she was 16 she quit school and moved to Los Angeles to start acting classes. She had a brief affair with Warren Beatty when she was still 16— although she told him she was older. But her life would change forever when she went on a double date with her boyfriend and her roommate one night and met Sonny Bono.

As Cher tells it, 'I was fascinated by Son from the moment he walked through the door … I actually thought to myself, "Something is different now. You're never going to be the same."' She was right. Although he wasn't interested in her straightaway—she was still 16—she moved into his apartment when she was kicked out of her own, an arrangement in which she was supposed to cook and clean in exchange for having a place to stay. He claimed he didn't find her attractive, and they slept in twin beds on opposite sides of the bedroom.

Cher hero-worshipped Sonny. When her mother discovered that she was living with this older man, she took her back to the family home. This was the catalyst for the change in their relationship: they missed each other, and Cher's mother had to resign herself to the relationship. As Sonny later recalled, 'She always had this mystique about her'.

When Sonny scored a job working for legendary record producer Phil Spector, he discovered Cher could sing, and she was soon doing backing vocals on Spector recordings, such as 'Da Doo Ron Ron' by the Ronettes and 'You've Lost That Lovin' Feelin'' by the Righteous Brothers. Sonny was writing his own material too, and was keen to harness Cher's unique voice. They started

playing live shows as a duo and then hit the jackpot with Sonny's song 'I Got You Babe'. It soared up the charts in 1965 and sold an astonishing three million copies. Suddenly they were stars.

A few more hit songs followed, and some unsuccessful films, but by the late 1960s the success had dried up. After four miscarriages, Cher and Sonny finally had a child: Chastity Sun Bono, born in 1969. The threesome began a difficult period touring the club circuit, and then were offered their own TV show. *The Sonny and Cher Comedy Hour* ran from 1971 to 1974. It was enormously successful, but behind the scenes there were problems. Cher and Sonny were both apparently having affairs. In Cher's words, 'We were a great team in every sense of the word. But fame, work, marriage and life get complicated.' The end of the show coincided with the end of the couple's marriage and their creative partnership. Apart from a brief revival of the TV show a couple of years later, Sonny and Cher, the entity, was no more. But they would remain friends until his death.

Cher remarried, this time to musician Greg Allman. The relationship was very brief but Cher had a son, Elijah. The late 1970s were not altogether successful—her solo albums were unsuccessful and her marriage fell apart. She changed her name, officially, to just 'Cher', and turned to acting. Her first major film role was alongside Meryl Streep in *Silkwood*, and she was nominated for an Academy Award for Best Supporting Actress for her performance. Four years later she won Best Actress for her role in *Moonstruck* with Nicholas Cage.

After several more film successes, she turned back to music, reinventing herself in the late 1980s and in the late 1990s.

> *'We were a great team in every sense of the word. But fame, work, marriage and life get complicated.'*

As for her relationship with Sonny, they never lost touch—and Chastity was always there to bind them together. Of Cher's successes after their break-up, Sonny once said, 'You've got to give someone like Cher a lot of credit. She's worked very hard to get where she is. I can't take that away from her'. In 1988 they appeared together on *The Late Show with David Letterman*, and were persuaded to sing 'I Got You Babe', more than 20 years after they had released the song. As Cher remembered it, 'It was like Son and I had never split up; we didn't miss a beat'. She talked later of the reunion as a very emotional one—audience members were crying; even Sonny's wife, Mary, had tears in her eyes; and Sonny looked like he was struggling himself. Cher remembers trying to hold herself together and feeling guilt and regret.

Sonny by this time had two children with his wife Mary, and a flourishing career as a restaurant owner. Later he would become mayor of Palm Springs in California, and then a congressman. But just as Cher was reaching another peak of success with her hit single 'Believe' in 1998, Sonny died suddenly in a skiing accident. Even though they had not been a couple since the mid-1970s, Cher felt the loss greatly, breaking down when she delivered the eulogy at his funeral.

Since then, Cher has shown no signs of dropping the pace, with a series of international concert tours and more films in production for future release. But she's never denied Sonny's role in her achievements: 'Son was the person who made Sonny and Cher possible ... In my life, at one time or another, he filled almost every role—father, brother, mentor, husband, partner, pain in the ass'. But despite her beginnings as Sonny Bono's other half, Cher was smart and talented enough to build a career far beyond her earliest days in the spotlight, and make a new name—just one name—all for herself.

Imelda Marcos

Known throughout the world for her obsession with expensive shoes, the former First Lady of the Philippines, Imelda Marcos, became as notoriously famous as her husband, President Ferdinand. As the couple ruled the country with an iron fist, Imelda's obsession with expensive luxury items, particularly shoes, and her role in corruption, earned her the nickname Steel Butterfly.

IMELDA ROMUALDEZ was born in 1929 on the island of Leyte. Her uncle, Norberto Romualdez Sr, served in the Philippine Supreme Court during the American era. In The Philippines' capital, Manila, in her twenties she exploited her beauty to advantage, among other things by putting herself forward to sing for American General Douglas Macarthur at the end of World War II. She then became a beauty queen in the 1950s, but failed to win the competition for Miss Manila in 1953.

In 1954 she met and married Ferdinand Marcos, a rich lawyer who was attracting attention as a rising political star. Manilans refer to the courtship as an 'eleven-day whirlwind', but the Marcoses married just three days after getting to know each other. The attractive couple soon became the centre of attention among the powerful, ruling elite in the post-colonial Philippines. The Spanish and American colony only became fully independent at the end of World War II.

Ferdinand was a cunning and ruthless political operator. In 1939 he had been convicted and jailed for the murder of one of his father's political opponents. He studied law and mounted his own appeal to the Supreme Court, successfully overturning his conviction in 1940.

Marcos entered the army for the duration of the war, but little is known of his activities. He apparently fabricated claims of being a highly decorated guerrilla fighter in World War II—claims which were part of the Marcos legend and central to his early popularity. These were discredited when US military documents were released in 1986.

In 1949 Ferdinand Marcos was elected to the Philippines House of Representatives and, in 1959, he won a seat in the Senate. Imelda was his most enthusiastic campaigner, bursting into song

whenever possible and always visible in her flamboyant outfits, expensive jewellery and big hair. In 1965 Marcos switched parties in a last minute pre-election deal and secured the presidency. With Imelda always by his side the new leader pledged to fight corruption and communism. *Time* magazine praised his 'dynamic, selfless leadership', and *Life* magazine compared Imelda to former American First Ladies, Jackie Kennedy and Eleanor Roosevelt. The couple resided like royalty in the Malacanang Palace in Manila, where they raised three children: Imee Marcos Manotoc, Irene Marcos Araneta and Ferdinand 'Bongbong' Marcos Jr.

Imelda took an active role in politics and took on significant portfolios such as Minister of Human Settlements and Governor of Metro Manila. She ordered the construction of several landmarks, including the Cultural Centre of the Philippines and the Manila Film Centre, which was rushed to completion at the cost of dozens of construction workers' lives. Ferdinand's 'creative diplomacy' apparently included using his wife as a sexual lure to elicit foreign contracts.

> *'I had to be a star for the poor people and, at the same time, I had to be a slave. I had to enslave myself so that everybody became a star.'*

With the war in Vietnam escalating, The Philippines was an important military base and staging post for the Americans, who poured billions of dollars into the local economy. Marcos appeared to be a benevolent and socially motivated president for the first few years. The ruling couple spent money on public works: hospitals, schools and airports. Imelda had her own pet projects including regal museums and luxury hotels. Imelda started social welfare programs and encouraged the 'Green Revolution' to increase agricultural production. When natural disasters struck, the people looked to the 'Mother of the Nation' for relief and assistance. The people were unaware that the couple were simultaneously cementing deals with the ruling families and funnelling millions of dollars of public funds into secret accounts and investments.

Much of the Marcos' fortune was syphoned off from state funds, war reparations from Japan and economic investments from America. Foreign aid appears to have been redirected for Imelda's personal requirements. The couple also institutionalised the practice of soliciting bribes and commissions in return for government employment, contracts, licences, concessions, permits, franchises and monopolies.

Imelda saw herself as a star, and flew around the globe in search of the most fashionable, custom-made shoes and was always turned out like a film star in gaudy jewellery and expensive dresses. She later justified her extravagance, claiming ,'I had to be a star for the poor people and, at the same time, I had to be a slave. I had to enslave myself so that everybody became a star.'

Her need for adulation was so great that in 1966 she demanded the visiting group The Beatles be brought to her home to entertain guests at a late-night party. When woken by the military police, their manager, Brian Epstein, refused and under siege by outraged Filipinos The Beatles were forced to flee the country.

Marcos was elected to a second—and legally final—term in office in 1969. The country's constitution forbade a president seeking a third term. He used the threat of terrorism and anarchy to seize total control of the country in 1972, suspending the constitution and dismissing the elected representatives. Once the constraints of democracy were removed and they held exclusive power, the Marcos' true colours emerged. The extent of their corruption was breathtaking. Working closely with the greedy elite, they plundered the country of any economic benefit it had derived from the heyday of the Vietnam war. This didn't seem to bother the American administration: ten years after Marcos seized dictatorial power, President George Bush Senior praised him for his 'adherence to democratic principles and the democratic process.'

Finally, after the assassination of leading opposition leader Benito Aquino by Marcos' military in 1986, the 'People's Power Revolution' swept the country and the couple were forced to flee when it became clear that the army no longer supported them. In the evening of 25 February, the Marcoses and their entourage left the presidential palace in four helicopters. Minutes later a swarm of protestors clambered over the gates and stormed the palace, which had been closed to the public for over a decade.

Imelda and Ferdinand didn't leave empty handed, flying into Hawaii with bags full of diamonds, gold bricks and certificates for a fortune in gold bullion. Estimates of the amount they squirrelled away are as high $35 billion. The Philippines national debt was about $28 billion at the time.

Imelda and Ferdinand didn't leave The Philippines empty handed, flying into Hawaii with bags full of diamonds, gold bricks and certificates for a fortune in gold bullion.

The impoverished citizens of the country soon discovered how soundly they had been betrayed: searching the palace, the citizens of Manila discovered five rooms full of Imelda's shoes— over 1200 pairs. In an extraordinary statement, Imelda unblinkingly used this to defend her husband's regime from charges of brutality and murder. 'The shoes', she declared, 'are my best defence, because when they went to my closet to look for skeletons, they found no skeletons, they only found shoes.'

Hounded by the media and courts, Ferdinand Marcos died in exile in 1989, shortly before a planned trial in New York. Imelda, true to form, found strength in adversity … and the wealth

A pro-Marcos rally in 1986.

that was now hers alone. She returned to the Philippines in 1992 from exile in Hawaii and campaigned for the presidency, promising to spend some of her ill-gotten gains on projects for the people. She failed, but in 1993 she convinced the Philippines' government to allow Ferdinand's embalmed body to be put on permanent display in Manila.

Imelda still refuses to apologise for the past, claiming that it's her family who deserves an apology. When confronted about her extravagances and the missing billions she feigns outrage, baldly stating, 'If you give it back, it means you've stolen it.'

In 1995 she won a seat in House of Representatives. The Steel Butterfly of the Philippines has no intention of leaving the stage just yet. At the age of 76 she can stand in front of the people and state: 'I'm still here.'

Speaking Out
1980-1989

Corazón Aquino

Cory Aquino was catapulted into the limelight after her husband Ninoy was assassinated in 1983 in The Philippines. Cory then rose to power to become the nation's President.

MARIA CORAZÓN SUMULONG COJUANGCO was born in Manila in 1933 into a wealthy and politically active family, the Cojuangcos of Tarlac province. She was educated in Manila and America at exclusive Catholic girls schools and eventually graduated with a Bachelor of Arts with a French major from Mount St Vincent's College in New York. At school the nuns taught Cory to be humble and 'that you must never do anything where your husband would lose face'. In 1953 she returned to The Philippines to begin a law degree at the Far Eastern University but abandoned her studies in 1955 at the age of 21 to marry Benigno (Ninoy) Aquino Jnr.

Ninoy and Cory first met when they were nine at a birthday party for his father, who was, like her father, a congressman. When she came home to Manila during her junior year at college she was impressed by the now older Ninoy as an intelligent and articulate young man. He was by then a young journalist of note and they began corresponding—Cory says she liked his letters as they were not 'mushy'. Their grand wedding brought together two of The Philippines, most powerful families, the land-owning Sumulongs and the politically influential Aquinos.

After they married, Ninoy was elected mayor of Concepcion, a quiet town outside of Manila. During these first years Cory promised her husband she would not pursue a career of her own nor play any role in his political life. She supported Ninoy's career, helping him campaign for governor and for his seat in the senate. Eventually, behind the scenes, she became a major influence on developing his 'People's Power' political doctrine.

Ninoy was famously critical of the Marcos regime and when martial law was declared he was promptly arrested on trumped-up charges of murder, illegal possession of firearms and subversion. For eight years, Cory was a regular visitor to the Bonafacio prison and acted as the point of contact between Ninoy and his supporters. She said this time was 'the making of the new Cory Aquino', the one who would later stand up as President. In 1980 Marcos exiled Ninoy and Cory and their family to the United States. Cory has described their time in Boston as one of the happiest times of her life, 'a second honeymoon', and it was during this time that they developed their ideas about effecting peace and freedom through non-violent revolution.

In 1983 Ninoy returned from exile and was assassinated almost as soon as he stepped off the plane. Although it was never officially proved, his assassin is said to have been Rolando Galman, who was immediately gunned down by troops. It is commonly thought to have been someone within the Marcos regime who organised the killing; some even say it was Imelda Marcos herself.

Ninoy's murder polarised popular opinion against the Marcos dictatorship and the spotlight shone brightly on his grieving widow, Cory. At first she thought public interest would subside and she would retreat into the background to fight Marcos from the sidelines. But when Ferdinand Marcos called a snap election at the end of 1985, Cory reluctantly agreed to head the opposition UNIDO party against him. She said of her decision retrospectively: 'We had to present somebody who was the complete opposite of Marcos, someone who had been a victim … Looking around, I may not be the worst victim, but I am the best-known'.

> *'I'm a woman but I'm ready to lay down my life for my country. I will restore honesty and sincerity in government.'*

Corazon Aquino gave her occupation on her certificate of candidacy as 'housewife'. Marcos criticised her political inexperience and her sex, but to no avail—she stood in perfect contrast to the years of corruption and material excess that characterised the Marcos family and that had alienated the Filipino people. Addressing one provincial village she said, 'I'm a woman but I'm ready to lay down my life for my country. I will restore honesty and sincerity in government.' Both Marcos and Aquino declared victory in the 1986 election, prompting what is now known as the 'People Power Revolution' or 'EDSA' which resulted in the Marcos family fleeing the archipelago for the islands of Hawaii.

When she came to power she worked at restoring the democratic institutions Marcos had destroyed: designing a new constitution to deter future dictatorships; addressing the problems of communist and Muslim uprisings; liberating political prisoners; and pursuing economic recovery.

Her time as president was difficult, and for the six years from 1986 to 1992, President Aquino had to toughen up to survive challenges from Marcos loyalists, communist insurrectionists and attempted military coups. Her presidency is best remembered by her wish to 'lead by example', her final gesture being to travel from her successor's inauguration in an ordinary Toyota Crown rather than the government-issued Mercedes, to signal her return to normal citizenry.

Corazón Aquino has become a role model for other Asian women leaders inspired by her non-violent model of revolution. She continues to have considerable political influence in The Philippines and her opinion are highly prized by politicians on both sides of the spectrum.

Sarah Brightman

Sarah Brightman rocketed to fame when she married Mr Musical, Andrew Lloyd Webber, and became his muse for the smash hit Phantom of the Opera. *Their very public divorce was by no means the end of her story as Sarah has reinvented her career with startling results.*

SARAH BRIGHTMAN was born on 14 August 1960 in Berkhampstead in the middle-class county of Hertfordshire in England. She was eldest of six children. She started to dance at the age of three, and 10 years later made her London theatrical debut in Charles Strouse's *I and Albert*. From a very young age, Sarah had a burning ambition to be famous. In 1976, she joined the famous dance group Pan's People on *Top of the Pops* the successful UK television chart show. At 16 she became a member of pop group Hot Gossip, a mixed dance act whose single 'I Lost my Heart to a Starship Trooper,' went straight to number one in 1978. Yet she was still relatively unknown.

In 1979 she married music producer Andrew Graham-Stewart, but three years later the couple divorced. She then auditioned for the role that would change her life—Jemima in the musical *Cats* at the New London Theatre. It was here she first met the show's composer, Andrew Lloyd Webber. The pair fell in love, despite the fact that Andrew was married. He divorced his wife and in 1984, married Sarah. He cast her as the lead, Christine Daaé, in his *Phantom Of The Opera*, said to have been written especially for her, alongside Michael Crawford. She also appeared in his *Requiem* and *Aspects of Love*.

Sarah's haunting and accurate voice was a perfect interpretation of Lloyd Webber's music. She released a number of solo albums, including 1988's *The Trees They Grow So High*, 1989's *The Songs That Got Away*, and *As I Come of Age* in the 1990s. But the critics slammed her work, not giving her the credit she felt she deserved and saying that the only reason for her success was that she was the wife of Lloyd Webber.

'It was such a creative time,' Sarah said of this period. 'Everything was happening very fast. Andrew was writing, I was singing. He was inspired, and I was inspired. I didn't really have time to think about it. I didn't really have time to read things about it, either. I got a sense of things, which made me quite nervous at times. But, no, we were running all the time then, doing things.

Sarah Brightman and Michael Crawford in Andrew Lloyd Webber's musical, The Phantom of the Opera.

It was fun, but also a lot of pressure.'

That pressure led to their divorce in 1990, while Sarah was completing her summer concert tour of *The Music of Andrew Lloyd Webber.*

Sarah was intimidated by the poor press and the lack of support she received from the London media. Escaping the media lens, she went to the United States and then Germany, where she met Frank Peterson from hit group Enigma in 1991. Frank went on to compose and produce all her music, making her famous all over the world.

Frank also re-invented Sarah's musical image, emphasising the cool. In 1993 success came with her first Peterson hit 'Captain Nemo', on the water-themed album *Dive.* Peterson persuaded Sarah to take opera singing lessons and her 1994 recording of 'Time to Say

Sarah with Andrew Lloyd Webber.

Goodbye' with opera star Andrea Bocelli (from the album of the same name), quickly became the biggest selling single in German recording history. It sold more than 4 million copies worldwide.

After *Dive*, Sarah recorded the album *Fly* in 1995 and *Eden* in 1998. She also released *The Andrew Lloyd Webber Collection*, which featured some of her memorable moments from Lloyd Webber cast recordings. *La Luna* followed in the spring of 2000; *Encore* the next year. Brightman then adopted a Middle Eastern theme for her 2003 release, *Harem.*

People who had never listened to opera before were being attracted to the genre through Sarah and her opera/pop influence. The first single off the American edition of *La Luna* was 'A Whiter Shade of Pale', remixed by German club and trance music producer Andre Tannenberger—making Sarah not just popular in mainstream music but also in the dance charts.

Sarah is so dedicated to her work that she has admitted going to the movies at midnight so it does not disturb her work during the day.

In 2003, Sarah launched a worldwide tour, performing 60 shows in the one year. The following year the Live From Las Vegas DVD and CD was released. She lives in Germany with Frank and spends time in Milan, training with her vocal teacher.

Katia Gordeeva

Katia has been classed as one of the top ten Winter Olympic athletes of all time. She was twice Olympic champion in pairs figure skating with her husband, Sergei Grinkov, before tragedy struck on the ice. Katia rebuilt her life, becoming a brilliant solo skater, best-selling author and mother, and is now married to Olympic skating gold medallist, Ilia Kulik.

EKATERINA ALEXANDROVNA GORDEEVA was born in 1971 in Moscow, Russia. She began skating when she was four and her talent was soon recognised. The Soviet Union had used sports as a tool to bolster national pride for some time, and when Josef Stalin decided to beat the West at its own game, the Soviet Union rapidly became one of the big Olympic medal winners.

Ekaterina, nicknamed Katia, was identified as a talent at school and sent to the rigorous skating training centre at the Central Red Army Club in Moscow. At age ten she was paired with 14-year-old Sergei Grinkov—a partnership that would take them to the heights of world skating fame. At the training centre, Katia faced intense competition and jealousy. She also despised the coach, Stanislav Alexeyvich Zhuk, who trained them in 1985. He was an alcoholic and abusive, and Gordeeva says in her book *My Sergei* that he beat and sexually harassed several female skaters. Finally the skaters rallied to get him demoted—no mean feat as he was a Soviet army colonel.

Despite the harshness of the regime, Katia and Sergei learned to move flawlessly together on the ice. In 1984, the duo won the Junior World Ice Skating Championships in Colorado Springs, USA, their first major victory together. After that they won virtually every competition they entered. Their talent powered them into the World Championships, in the aftermath of the success of Jayne Torvill and Christopher Dean. Katia and Sergei won the title in 1986 and again in 1987.

Katia was tiny in comparison to Sergei, but their dramatic difference in size helped them to perform a variety of complex lifts and throws. They are one of the few couples in history to successfully complete a quadruple twist lift in international competition.

The pair began training intensely for the 1988 Olympic Winter Games in Calgary, Canada. In 1988, G&G, as they had become known, captured the gold medal in their very first Olympic competition, and that same year their relationship blossomed into romance. Katia and Sergei

became known for their technical excellence and their ability to relate to one another and the music while performing. Turning professional in 1990, they began working with choreographer Marina Zueva. Marina is Katia's choreographer today and the two have a close relationship. In 1991 Katia and Sergei won their first World Professional Championships, and won the title again in 1992 and 1994.

Katia married Sergei in April 1991. The following season was the first year they became professional and toured with Disney's *Stars on Ice*. On 11 September 1992, Katia gave birth to their daughter, Daria Sergeevna Grinkova (nicknamed 'Dasha'). Shortly after the birth, Katia was back on the ice training for the new season of *Stars on Ice*, which debuted that November.

In 1992 the rules governing professionals entering the Olympics changed, opening the way for G&G to compete. Katia and Sergei captured their second gold medal at the 1994 Winter Olympics in Lillehammer, Norway. They then returned to professional skating and took up residence in the United States. During the 1994-95 season they toured again with *Stars on Ice*, this time as headliners. That year, Katia was named one of the '50 Most Beautiful People' by *People Magazine*.

In 1995 tragedy struck. While skating on the *Stars on Ice* practice rink in Lake Placid, New York, 28-year-old Sergei had a heart attack and died an hour later. Katia was devastated. The pair were so inextricably linked, her skating was identified so strongly with his, that the skating community found it hard to imagine how her life could go on without him. But Katia bravely took to the ice again. Skating alone in February 1996, her first performance was a tribute to her late husband. The same year, with author EM Swift, she told the story of her life in *My Sergei: A Love Story*.

Katia found solace in an international skating community that was also shaken by Grinkov's sudden death. They rallied around her. 'During that time [the skating community] was very supportive, and they knew the story, and they knew me and Sergei ... so it was nice [to have] good, close friends,' she told CNN. 'To come back on the ice was hard, and at the same time it was kind of a healing process,' she said.

In February 1998, the CBS television network aired her story based on the book, and in April her second book was published under the title *A Letter for Daria*. Katia's solo skating career has blossomed with *Stars on Ice*. She and Daria appeared in the 1997 Christmas movie *Snowden on Ice* and Katia appeared in the 1998 sequel *Snowden's Raggedy Ann* and *The Andy Holiday Show*.

In 1998, at the Winter Olympics in Japan, Katia met the men's gold medallist, Ilia Kulik. They skated together in a tour of 1998 and fell in love. In 2001 she gave birth to their daughter, Elizaveta Ilyinichna Kulik (nicknamed 'Liza'). They married in a private ceremony in San Francisco in 2002.

Katia and Ilia live in Connecticut and train at the International Skating Center there. While her Olympic gold medals remain dear to her, she says that her children are her greatest accomplishment. 'Family is always the most important part,' she said.

Diana, Princess of Wales

She outshone her husband in every way and was able to use her fame to further countless charitable causes. But she also paid a terrible price for her celebrity, and the damage it wrought on her was unprecedented.

DIANA SPENCER was born in 1961, becoming Lady Diana when her father inherited his earldom in 1975. She grew up in a house on one of the estates of Queen Elizabeth, with the young princes Andrew and Edward as her playmates. She attended schools in the counties of Norfolk and Kent, then capped off her education at a Swiss finishing school. When she returned to London, she began working at an exclusive kindergarten as a teacher, and re-entered the royal circles she'd grown up in. It was only a matter of time before she came into contact with Prince Charles.

Reports of Prince Charles' friendship with a young, shy, beautiful woman first appeared in 1980. Charles met Diana at a polo match, and had found her conversation interesting and direct. He was more than 10 years her senior, and had been engaged in many publicised affairs—most notably with Camilla Parker Bowles. His relationship with Diana progressed, and press photographers began staking out the kindergarten where Diana worked, forcing her to leave the job. In early 1981, the couple became engaged. Their wedding in July 1981 saw tens of millions of television viewers tuned in worldwide. The Diana phenomenon was well underway.

Because it was such a public relationship, the rumours started almost immediately. Diana said later that their early days were difficult but happy: 'I desperately wanted it to work, I desperately loved my husband and I wanted to share everything together, and I thought that we were a very good team'. She had some assistance from royal advisers on dealing with the media, but the level of the attention was not easy to handle. The couple's first child, William, was born in June 1982, and Diana suffered post-natal depression, later admitting to self-harming during this period. It was the first hint that the 21-year-old princess was finding her new lifestyle psychologically destructive. By the time their second child, Harry, was born in 1984, Diana's problems were worsening. She became bulimic, a condition the royal family knew about but didn't understand.

As Diana put it, 'It was a symptom of what was going on in my marriage. I was crying out for help, but giving the wrong signals'. Charles had renewed his relationship with Camilla Parker Bowles,

and Diana was soon having her own affairs, most notably with James Hewitt. She later claimed that she and Charles had a mutual understanding about these extramarital relationships.

Diana recognised her fame brought opportunities for publicising social causes. In 1987, she opened Britain's first dedicated AIDS ward in a London hospital, shaking hands with patients at a time when people believed the disease was transferable by simple skin contact. 'HIV does not make people dangerous to know,' she said at the time, 'so you can shake their hands or give them a hug. God knows they need it.' It was said that the Queen did not approve of Diana taking up this cause, but it endeared her to the British public.

Her relationship with Charles was, however, falling apart. The pressure on their marriage was hard to bear. Diana suggested that 'basically we were a married couple doing the same job, which is very difficult for anyone, and more so if you've got all the attention on you'. In 1992, the pressure finally overloaded the marriage and Diana and Charles separated. A tell-all biography of Diana was published. The Queen called that year her *annus horribilis*.

Diana continued her charity work but in a reduced capacity. She gave a much-publicised television interview on the BBC's *Panorama* program in late 1995, where she admitted her affair with James Hewitt and said that Charles' love for Camilla Parker Bowles was a constant factor: 'there were three of us in this marriage, so it was a bit crowded'. The interview caused a public furore. She did, however, claim that her reaction to the separation was 'deep, deep, profound sadness'.

When her divorce from Charles was finalised in 1996, Diana dropped patronage of about 100 of her charities, keeping only a handful, including the National AIDS Trust. She also took an interest in the Red Cross landmines project, making a trip to Angola to visit victims. In mid-1997, rumours began circulating that she was to marry Dodi Al Fayed, the son of a wealthy Egyptian businessman. After a night at the Paris Ritz on 31 August, Dodi and Diana were being driven at speed through Paris in an attempt to evade press photographers. In one of the tunnels under the city, the driver crashed their car into a concrete pillar. He died instantly, as did Dodi. Diana suffered internal bleeding and several cardiac arrests, and was pronounced dead a few hours later. The driver was found to have well over the legal limit of alcohol in his system.

The whole of Britain, it seemed, went into mourning for Diana. A sea of floral tributes were left at the gates of Buckingham and Kensington Palaces. Charles organised the funeral in conjunction with Prime Minister Tony Blair, as the protocols for a royal funeral did not apply. People camped out for days to get a view of the funeral procession, and the event was televised for millions of viewers.

Since her death, Diana's fame has been cemented in history by countless books, television documentaries, articles and public discussion. Charles may still be the heir to the British throne, but it is Diana's children who will follow him, and it is her memory that lives on in the mind of the public.

Camilla, Duchess of Cornwall

The Duchess of Cornwall is the classic royal mistress. Once hated by the British for being the 'third person' in the marriage of Charles and Diana, Camilla has now inherited the role of royal wife and is winning the fight for the public's approval.

CAMILLA SHAND, NICKNAMED MILLA, was born on 17 July 1947 into an upper class British family. She was educated at Queen's Gate School in South Kensington, London, and attended finishing school in Switzerland. And at the age of 25, she met Prince Charles at Windsor Great Park in the early 1970s, and the two became friends. She told him she was a descendant of Alice Keppel, who became King Edward VII's mistress when he was Prince of Wales. Prince Charles was immediately captivated by her, describing her later as a 'breath of fresh air'.

Camilla was sexy and outspoken and shared his love of dogs, horses and the countryside. They started a relationship that lasted until the following year, 1971, when Charles joined the Royal Navy. Charles was in no rush to marry and Camilla accepted the marriage proposal of Andrew Parker Bowles, a handsome cavalry officer who had previously dated Princess Anne, Charles' sister. Camilla and Charles remained close friends—legend has it that Camilla helped the prince choose Lady Diana Spencer as a suitable wife. It is even rumored that Charles proposed to Diana in the Parker Bowles' vegetable garden.

Diana called Camilla the 'rottweiler', and some claim Charles and Camilla were having an affair throughout his marriage. Diana said there were three in their marriage, making it 'a little crowded'. Charles and Diana separated in 1992 but didn't divorce until 1996. Some say Camilla moved into Highgrove House with Charles after her own divorce in 1995. Two years later, in 1997, Charles publicly hosted a fiftieth birthday party for Camilla, raising her profile and helping her to gain public acceptance.

Young Camilla and Charles at a polo match in the 1970s.

A month later, Princess Diana and her lover Dodi al-Fayed were killed in a car crash in Paris. The public outpouring of grief was overwhelming and drove Camilla underground.

After two years, Charles and Camilla were seen out together again, at her sister Annabel's fiftieth birthday. Camilla began to accompany Charles to public events. They shared their first public kiss and Camilla won his children's approval, his mother's approval, and finally the approval of the public. It wasn't easy—Camilla was once belted with bread rolls by supermarket shoppers—but gradually, with her charity work she first won over the media and then the public. The nation received news of their wedding in 2005 with warmth and thousands of Britons offered their congratulations in the form of cards and flowers. The two Princes, Harry and William, were pleased and issued a statement saying so.

The world watched as Camilla became the Duchess of Cornwall at Windsor Castle in April 2005. Twenty thousand well wishers turned up. William and Harry said they were 'very happy' and wished the couple 'all the luck in the world'. Even though he was marrying a divorcee, which her uncle had abdicated the throne to do, Queen Elizabeth approved, issuing a statement that said: 'The Duke of Edinburgh and I are very happy that the Prince of Wales and Mrs Parker Bowles are to marry'.

Camilla now accompanies Charles on royal tours and when he represents the Queen on state visits. She is known as the Princess Consort—which means that should Charles ever be king, Camilla will not inherit her husband's titles and privileges. The Duchess now also undertakes her own solo duties. She is the patron of the National Osteoporosis Society (her mother died from the disease). She attended the Trooping the Colour ceremony in London for the first time in June 2005, and made her first appearance on the balcony of Buckingham Palace afterwards.

After the 7 July 2005 London bombings, Camilla accompanied Prince Charles to visit victims of the attack at St Mary's Hospital in Paddington. In November 2005, she accompanied Prince Charles on a royal tour of the United States, her first official international tour as a member of the British Royal Family. Finally, the mistress has become the wife.

Jerry Hall

When Jerry Hall divorced Rolling Stone Mick Jagger it looked like she would fade from the public gaze. But the tall, blond, supermodel won over the public by reinventing herself as a single mother, strengthening her career and even keeping a friendly relationship with her tempestuous ex.

JERRY HALL was born Jerry Faye, a twin with Terry Jaye, in 1956 in Gonzalez, Texas. When she was two, the family moved to Mesquite, a nearby Texan working-class town. She was born into a dysfunctional family, often facing the wrath of her alcoholic father, a truck driver who would dose himself up with amphetamines to keep himself awake. Hall said, 'He would come home and hit us and scream at us, and I lived in fear of him throughout most of my childhood.'

Jerry went to North Mesquite High School and when she was 16, left home with one suitcase to pursue a modelling career in Paris and at nearly 6ft (182 cm) tall, with waist-length blonde hair, she did well. She first came into the public eye when she became engaged to the lead singer of Roxy Music, Bryan Ferry. A cover girl, the face of Yves Saint Laurent Opium perfume and Revlon cosmetics, Jerry also starred in two of Roxy Music's videos, and posed for the sleeve of their 1975 album *Sirens*. When she was 20, Jerry met Rolling Stones front man, Mick Jagger, in 1976. They became an item and five years later Jerry gave birth to Elizabeth Scarlett. Their son, James Leroy Augustin, was born in 1985. 'Mick told me he read somewhere that rock stars have breakdowns because they lose touch with reality,' Jerry said in 1985. 'He said he was thinking about it the other day when he was loading up the station wagon with baby stuff and said, "There's no fear of that now".'

While Jerry's modelling career took a back seat, she remained a magnet for photographers whenever she was out. Over the next decade she landed small roles in films such as 1989's *Batman*, and *Princess Caraboo* in 1994. In 1988, when someone asked her when she would marry Mick, who famously said marriage gave him 'claustrophobia', Jerry exclaimed: 'Golly, I'm tryin'! Y'all quit rubbin' it in!' They finally tied the knot on 21 November, 1990, in Bali, and their third child, Georgia May Ayeesha, soon followed. In 1997 Jerry gave birth to her fourth baby, Gabriel.

Jerry has an interesting attitude to women's bodies, considering her glamour model status. She

was a positive advocate of breastfeeding and was on the front cover of *Vanity Fair* magazine in a glamorous Annie Leibovitz photograph breastfeeding Gabriel. She has also spoken out against plastic surgery, saying that it's an 'illness' that turns people into 'monsters'.

When Gabriel was two, model Luciana Morad announced she was pregnant with Mick's child. Jerry had put up with Mick's womanising for a long time, but this was too much. She filed for divorce, hiring Mishcon de Reya, the firm that represented Princess Diana in her divorce from Prince Charles. Her marriage to Mick was annulled by a High Court judge in 1999. Arguments about settlement and property were carried out in the full glare of the media, but Jerry came through it with dignity. After the divorce, Mick apologised to Jerry for his behaviour, blaming the lawyers.

Jerry continued modelling but now took more of an interest in acting. In 2000 she was congratulated for her theatrical performance as Mrs Robinson in *The Graduate*, replacing Hollywood star Kathleen Turner. Like her predecessor, Jerry appeared naked on stage as the middle-aged temptress. Prince Azim of Brunei gave her a diamond bracelet after he saw her in the role. She told the press that Jagger was babysitting their children while she was on stage—just as she had done while he was appearing on tour during their two decades together.

Since her divorce, she has gone out with millionaires and producers. She studied for an Open University degree in poetry. Her acting career has seen performances in the tiny Islington's Kings' Head pub theatre and in *Picasso's Women* at the Malvern Festival Theatre. She played Mother Lord in the London revival of Cole Porter's *High Society*. In 2005, she starred in the reality television series *Kept*, revolving around a competition for a 'kept' man to share in her life of luxury.

In 2003 she told the *Radio Times* that Mick Jagger 'needs help' for his womanising ways. She said that the rocker's lust was 'incurable'. 'I was brought up not to know what it's like to be treated well, which is probably why I stayed with Mick so long. I really tried for 25 years. I had the patience of a saint but he's an incurable womaniser—and not very discreet.'

Jerry insists Mick has been a good father and has always been supportive of her career. 'It confuses people that we get on so well,' she told *Hello!* magazine. 'We will never give up on the relationship we have as friends and parents.' Jerry and the children live in the 5 million pound family mansion in London's Richmond Hill.

Priscilla Presley

Priscilla Beaulieu stepped into the media glare when she married Elvis, the King of Rock and Roll. Surviving their divorce, his sickness and death, she maintained a cool sophistication, which stood her in good stead as she reinvented her life as actress, author, film producer and personality.

PRISCILLA ANN WAGNER was born on 24 May 1945, in Brooklyn, New York. Her father was James Wagner, a US Navy pilot. Her mother was a Norwegian-American, Anna Lillian Iversen. When James was killed in a plane crash when Priscilla was a child, Anna married Paul Beaulieu, a US Air Force officer, and Priscilla took his name. The Beaulieus were stationed in West Germany. At the same time the young rocker Elvis Presley, well known by that time, was stationed there during his stint in the US Army. Priscilla was 14 years old when she met and fell in love with Elvis, after being introduced to him by her friend and one of Elvis's army buddies, Currie Grant.

In her teens, Priscilla would fly to the United States to visit Elvis at Gracelands, the home he'd built, outside Memphis, California or Las Vegas, depending on where he was performing or filming. Elvis missed her when she returned to Germany to school and tried to talk the extremely reluctant Beaulieus into allowing young Priscilla to live with his father Vernon and his stepmother at a home Elvis purchased on Heritage Drive in Memphis.

Her mother finally agreed and her protective stepfather flew with her to Los Angeles in 1962 where Presley was filming *Fun in Acapulco*. After discussing the rules—no sleeping in the same bedroom—she and her stepfather flew to Memphis where they met with Vernon, made arrangements for Priscilla's enrolment in the Immaculate Conception School and confirmed her living arrangements. Priscilla was 17. Once in Memphis, Priscilla moved into Graceland bit by bit, at first spending occasional nights with Presley, later moving in. They were married on 1 May 1967 in Las Vegas when Priscilla was 22, at the Aladdin Hotel and Casino. On the first of February 1968, Priscilla gave birth to their only daughter, Lisa Marie.

Even though the world envied her position, Priscilla was miserable. In her 1985 book *Elvis and Me*, she described how Elvis suffered insomnia. Even in 1962 when she first moved to Graceland, he was taking sleeping pills. His behaviour became more erratic, drug dependent and

Priscilla, aged 16, sits in the backseat with Elvis Presley on his way to the airport at the end of his tour of duty in Germany in 1960.

abusive. He surrounded himself with other women and a sycophantic set of people, and would stay up all night and sleep all day. The pressures led to their 'amicable divorce' in 1973. They shared custody of their Lisa Marie, who lived in Los Angeles with Priscilla.

On 16 August 1977, Elvis died from heart failure. Devastated, Priscilla and Lisa Marie mourned with the rest of the world. But Priscilla did not retreat. After Elvis's death she opened a boutique store in Beverly Hills, was offered acting job and began to model. Her profile and career soared. When she landed the role of Jenna Wade on the internationally popular CBS Television series *Dallas*, Priscilla became one of its most popular leading ladies. She also proved she could be funny in the *Naked Gun* series, a box office smash from 1994 to 1991. She starred in the movie *Breakfast with Einstein*, and 1983's popular TV series *The Fall Guy*. She also guest-starred in back-to-back episodes of the award winning ABC Television comedy series *Spin City*.

Priscilla has always been committed to the memory of Elvis—she still loved him when they separated. She established herself as an author when she wrote the successful *Elvis and Me* which topped *The New York Times* bestseller list and become a television mini-series produced by her company, Navarone Productions. But she has moved on, and since 1984, has lived with Brazilian writer-director Marco Garibaldi. Their son Navarone was born on 1 March 1987. She sits on the board of directors of MGM and was executive producer on the feature film *Finding Graceland*, starring Harvey Keitel as Elvis.

At the same time, Priscilla has launched several perfumes and joined Hollywood celebrities in a fight against the overmedication of children. The young teenager has come a long way.

Paula Yates

Wild child Paula Yates lived dangerously. With two famous pop stars as partners—Bob Geldof and Michael Hutchence—she made her fair share of headlines, in her life and in her tragic death.

PAULA YATES WAS BORN ON 24 APRIL 1959. She was brought up in North Wales in a showbusiness family by her mother—former showgirl, actress and writer of erotic novels, Heller Thornton—and the television star Jess Yates—known as 'the Bishop', who presented the ITV religious program *Stars On Sunday*. Paula's father was 16 years older than his wife and their marriage was unconventional. In an unsettled childhood, from the age of eight Paula lived mostly with her mother, including spells in Malta and Majorca.

Arriving in London aged 16 she immersed herself in the punk scene, where she met Irish Boomtown Rats singer Bob Geldof—organiser of the 1985 and 2005 Band Aid and Live Aid famine relief events. Paula became an obsessed fan of the Rats in their early days and it wasn't long before she and Geldof got together as a couple. She was 17 and Geldof was 21. Paula and Bob married in 1986 and had three children: Fifi Trixibelle, Peaches Honeyblossom and Pixie.

With her peroxide-blonde hair, Paula came to media attention in the 1980s as co-presenter with Jools Holland of the British pop music program *The Tube*. She was also one of the presenters on *The Big Breakfast*, which was produced by Geldof. In 1995 Paula interviewed a young Australian rock singer, INXS front man Michael Hutchence, while lying in a bed on *The Big Breakfast*. She fell in love and left Geldof for him. A bitter and very public divorce battle followed, in which she lost custody of her three children—Paula had no chance when opium was reportedly discovered under her bed.

Newspapers laughed at the fact Michael had left his supermodel girlfriend Helena Christensen for Paula Yates and the couple's three-year relationship drew huge media interest Michael and Paula had a daughter together, Heavenly Hiraani Tiger Lily, known as Tiger Lily. Their relationship seemed to be passionate, sexy, yet stable—a couple truly, madly in love.

In 1997 tragedy struck when Hutchence was found hanged in a hotel room in Sydney. Paula was distraught, refusing to accept the coroner's verdict of suicide, saying he died accidentally in a sexual experiment that went tragically wrong. She was pictured in every magazine and newspaper

around the world as the black widow. She said at the time, 'He was the love of my life, the man I wanted to spend the rest of my days with.' Describing her torment to friends, she said she slept with her lover's ashes, and she told one friend she would be written about as 'a suicide blonde'.

Struggling to come to terms with Michael's death, Paula suffered depression and had a nervous breakdown, and surrendered to her long-running drug problems. She eventually sought psychiatric treatment and did a stint in drug rehabilitation.

The year after Michael's death there were reports that she had tried to hang herself, but was saved by a friend who found her slumped in the bedroom of her London home. She was barely conscious and had a noose around her neck. Media reports said it was a suicide attempt in a bid to copy Hutchence.

'She was a vibrant personality, she lived life to the full.
She epitomised the rock and roll lifestyle.'

Meanwhile, Michael Hutchence's Australian parents began a fight over custody of their granddaughter Tiger Lily, although his father was said to have been more of a peacemaker than a combatant. Neighbours around Paula's home in London's fashionable Notting Hill spoke about how she was frequently seen out with her daughter Tiger Lily and appeared cheerful and friendly. Then Paula took a final blow: the media revealed that Jess Yates had not been Paula's natural father. A paternity test proved that late quiz show host Hughie Green had been her biological father.

Shortly after this in 2000, on the tenth birthday of her daughter Pixie, Paula was found dead, at the age of 40, from an apparent drug overdose. Her death was recorded as the result of 'an unsophisticated taker of heroin using drugs'. A quantity of 0.3 mg of morphine per litre of blood was found in her body, which would not have been enough to kill her had she been a heroin addict. Detective Inspector Michael Christensen told the court that brown power containing heroin had been found on her bedside table, as well as a 5 pound note containing traces of cocaine.

Her solicitor, Mark Stephens, who handled her divorce, said: 'She was a vibrant personality, she lived life to the full. She epitomised the rock and roll lifestyle. Her children were the real passion of her life. She would quite often be at home with them rather than going to the opening of an envelope, as some people did. The blow of Michael's death hit her for six, it took all her energy to come back from that. She's now with the man that she loved, hopefully she'll be at peace.' After Yates's death, Bob Geldof became the legal guardian of Tiger Lily, believing that she should be raised with her three half-sisters.

Left: Paula arrives at Michael Hutchence's funeral with Tiger Lily in 1997.

Courtney Love

Courtney Love is an outspoken and controversial musician and actor, and the widow of Nirvana frontman Kurt Cobain. Although a talented musician with several well-regarded albums behind her, Courtney is today as famous for her court appearances and colourful public behaviour.

SEPARATING THE MYTH FROM THE REALITY of Courtney Love's life is not easy. Her own frank and contradictory media comments, the inflammatory books written by her mother and her estranged father, and the media frenzy surrounding Kurt Cobain's death, mixes soap opera, road movie and chilling nightmare. Born Courtney Harrison in San Francisco in 1964 to Hank Harrison, a one-time manager of the band the Grateful Dead, and Linda Risi, a psychologist, Courtney's childhood was by all accounts chaotic. Both she and her mother claim that Hank gave her LSD at the age of four. Within a few years she was living with her mother and a series of step-fathers in alternative communes; by age 12 she was drinking and was found self-harming. She was sent to a treatment centre from which she escaped, but was recaptured, landing in a reform school until she was 16. On her release, she broke with her family and began travelling around the United States, using money from a trust fund set up by her grandmother.

In the early 1980s that Courtney first appeared oin a very brief stint as lead singer of the band Faith No More. After her first appearance in a film (*Sid and Nancy*) in 1986, she formed the band Babes in Toyland but after arguing with her co-founder, was thrown out and began working as a stripper. In 1989 she formed her own band, Hole. Its first album, *Pretty on the Inside*, was not a runaway success. In 1990 she met Nirvana's Kurt Cobain and it wasn't long before they'd begun an intense relationship. United by music and reputed heavy drug use, Courtney and Kurt fast became a celebrity couple, with reports of their heroin habits and volatile behaviour. When they first met, Nirvana's *Bleach* album was being outsold by Hole's debut, but that changed dramatically with the release of Nirvana's defining album, *Nevermind*, in 1991. Kurt Cobain became one of the biggest rock stars in the world, and Courtney was riding the wave.

In early 1992, Courtney discovered she was pregnant, and the couple married in Hawaii. Their daughter, Frances Bean Cobain, was born in August 1992. But the marriage was already in trouble, and by 1993 Kurt had overdosed and possibly attempted suicide at least twice. When Courtney

admitted in a *Vanity Fair* article that she had used heroin while (unknowingly) pregnant with Frances, a publicity storm raged, despite her protests that she'd been misquoted. The couple was investigated by child welfare authorities. The stage was set for a tragedy.

In April 1994, Kurt was found in his home in Lake Washington, shot in the head, with an enormous amount of heroin in his bloodstream and an apparent suicide note by his side. The official verdict was that the death was a suicide. Some commentators mentioned conspiracy. Some commentators (including Courtney's estranged father) placed the blame on Courtney, even suggesting she hired someone to shoot Kurt (although there is no evidence to support this); others maintain that while their relationship was troubled, Kurt had a history of suicide threats.

> *'What's the fucking point if you don't have soaring heights of passion, moments of intensity and beauty? With Kurt, I was never bored'.*

In a *Rolling Stone* interview, Courtney discussed her sense of loss at the death of Kurt: 'I used to feel like mourning him was really selfish because it would make him feel guilty. And the best thing to do was to pray for him and show him joy. But now I know he's dissipated, and he's gone. There's not anything left'. A few months after his death, Hole released their most highly acclaimed album, *Live Through This*, which had been written and recorded before Kurt's death.

Courtney's Golden Globe-nominated performance in the film *The People Vs. Larry Flynt* in 1996 made her name as a talented actor. She feuded with Nirvana's remaining members over her controlling influence on the band's unreleased material. She championed musicians' rights in the music industry before suing her own record company. She also managed to become something of a fashion icon. Her solo musical career was set in motion with 'Celebrity Skin' in 2004.

In late 2003 she was arrested smashing windows in her ex-boyfriend's house under the influence of drugs. She lost custody of her daughter and faced criminal charges. Then, in 2004, she hit a clubgoer over the head with a microphone stand at a concert and was charged with assaulting a woman she confronted in the same ex-boyfriend's house. Courtney faced possible imprisonment and her lawyers were only able to keep her out of gaol as long as she served community service, attended anger management therapy and Narcotics Anonymous, and completed 18 months of drug rehabilitation. In January 2005 she regained custody of her daughter and has faced no new charges since 2004.

Of her relationship with Kurt, Courtney has said: 'What's the fucking point if you don't have soaring heights of passion, moments of intensity and beauty?...With Kurt, I was never particularly bored'.

Backlash and Enlightenment 1990-1999

Hazel Hawke

Hazel Hawke's marriage to Australian Prime Minister Bob Hawke gave her a public profile. Since their public divorce, Hazel has reclaimed her identity as a champion of social welfare.

BORN AND RAISED IN MOUNT HAWTHORN, PERTH—a 'battlers' suburb'—Hazel Masterson had a happy childhood. She was outgoing, shared a close relationship with her sister, and loved to play the piano. She also loved school, and was sad to leave when she was just 15: World War II was not yet over, and she was expected to work. She took a job as a shorthand typist and bookkeeper. She was also active in the local Congregational Church, and it was at one of their youth fellowship camps that she first encountered young Bob Hawke.

During the 1948 Easter camp, when they were both 18, Hazel liked what she saw: 'his eyes were a deep blue, his hair was luxuriously thick, dark brown and wavy'. In his memoirs, Bob recalled her as a 'vibrant girl', who had 'one of the most beautiful pairs of legs I had ever seen'. After the camp, Bob decided to ask 'one of the Mount Hawthorn girls' on an outing, and from a list of three he suggested to his mother, Ellie, she recommended Hazel. They went on the date, and quickly launched into an affair, the intensity of which surprised them both.

Together the 'Golden Couple', as their church friends called them, worked on church committees, went on holidays and spent time with each other's families. Bob was studying law, which increased his appeal for Hazel—she still felt she'd missed out on the university life. In 1950, Bob asked Hazel to marry him: 'How much I wanted to marry him! But I was afraid that I would not be adequate.' Bob's response surprised her: he said he wouldn't have wanted to marry her if she had been to university. He wanted a wife who would play a more traditional role. But they delayed their marriage—Bob was applying for a Rhodes scholarship at Oxford, and only single men could apply. In 1952 Hazel discovered she was pregnant. Abortion was illegal, but she felt she had no choice, or Bob's chances of a scholarship would be ruined. The termination of her pregnancy was a painful and traumatic experience that later made Hazel a firm campaigner for family planning and counselling services.

Bob received his Rhodes scholarship, and took off for Oxford. Hazel joined him sooner than

planned—Bob had written and asked her to come early in case he was tempted by the life of a single man. She found a secretarial job and they stayed until 1956, after which they returned to Perth and were married. Hazel was now a wife, and soon to be a mother. For the next 25 years, these would be Hazel's primary roles. She had three children by 1961, and a fourth child who died in 1963 at just four days old.

Hazel and Bob's relationship was often rocky, and by the late 1970s they were discussing whether they could stay together—Bob had always been a heavy drinker and a womaniser. But they stayed together, and Hazel eventually began volunteer work with the Brotherhood of St Laurence, cementing her interest in social welfare issues. Her visits to their son Stephen in the Kimberley, where he worked with Aboriginal communities, opened her eyes to indigenous issues. In 1980 she began studying for a diploma in welfare.

When Bob became Australian prime minister in 1983, Hazel quickly learned to use her position to support important social causes. She was involved in drug education, the environment, women's rights, education, domestic violence, issues facing migrants and Aboriginal people, children's causes and cancer research. In 1984, as the first prime minister's wife to be invited to give a National Press Club luncheon speech, she spoke about the problems facing Aboriginal people, immigrants and the poor. Her views on the position of women were unequivocal: 'Women must accept that with more equality they must take more responsibility for themselves, not copping out with the dumb blonde, or the dependent, or hard-done-by little woman syndromes'.

At home, Bob had given up drinking in 1980, but their youngest daughter, Ros, had become addicted to heroin. Hazel took care of the grandchildren while Ros went into rehabilitation in an American clinic. In 1989, Bob admitted in a television interview that he had been unfaithful to her. Public support for Hazel surged. In 1991, Bob lost the leadership of the Labor Party—and the prime ministership—and Hazel had an ovarian cyst and a tumour removed. Finally, in 1995, Bob announced their divorce, and married his biographer, Blanche d'Alpuget. Again, public support for Hazel, who had stood by Bob through all the worst times, was immense.

In 2001, the year she was awarded the Order of Australia, Hazel was also diagnosed with Alzheimer's disease. Her family went public with the news in 2003, and Hazel wrote a book with her daughter, Sue, about her struggle with the condition. She set up the Hazel Hawke Alzheimer's Research and Care Foundation to raise money for research.

Of her relationship with Bob, Hazel once said, 'My development as a woman began at the moment Bob and I set out together'. In many ways it is what she has done without Bob—for herself and those less fortunate than herself—that has made her such a highly esteemed Australian.

Annita Keating

Annita Keating rose to fame as the wife of former Australian Labor Party leader and Prime Minister Paul Keating. Her support for the arts, her grace and style made her an immediately attractive—not least as an antidote to the working class boy from Bankstown.

ANNA (ANNITA) JOHANNA MARIA VAN IERSEL was born in 1949 into a strict Catholic family in the Netherlands. Not many details of her life before meeting Paul Keating are in the public domain—it is well known that she became an air hostess for the Italian airline Alitalia, and that it was during the course of her flying career that she met Paul.

The story of how Annita was courted by her future husband Paul Keating is one of the few personal stories the couple have shared. He, then a Labor party backbencher, was flying first class to Bangkok, she was the hostess who caught his eye. Annita tells how Paul studied her for most of the flight but said nothing—it was only after disembarking that he decided to run back to the plane and give her his card. Three and a half years later, in January 1975, Annita married Paul in her family's village in Holland. She had swapped her Rome apartment and glamourous jet-set life for that of a Bankstown housewife in the outer suburbs of Sydney. Thus began what has been described as 'the toughest years of her life'.

In a rare 2004 interview with the Australian magazine *The Bulletin* Annita said of her early married life, 'I was a foreigner and had no friends. Paul didn't really have any friends who were really close. I was very isolated, it was very tough and I knew that if I would survive there, I would survive anything in life.' The isolation was exacerbated by the fact that Paul's mother, Nana Min, thought her son's new wife looked down her European nose on the family residence in the western suburbs of Sydney. During these hard years she did have one very strong source of joy, her children. She gave birth to three of her four children Patrick (1977), Caroline (1979) and Katherine (1982) while in Sydney; Alexandra (1985) was born in Canberra.

In 1983 Paul Keating became the Federal Treasurer in the newly elected Labor Government, and the family duly relocated to Canberra. Annita became firm friends with Hazel Hawke, the then prime minister Bob Hawke's wife, and 20 years older than herself. She learned much about political

life from Mrs Hawke and both women were regulars at the visitor's gallery at Parliament House.

Annita's friendship with Hazel became strained when in 1991 Keating challenged Hawke for the Labor Party leadership and won. From then on, as Paul Keating became the prime minister in 1991, Annita was constantly in the public eye. She lent her name to a number of Cinderella causes. The first was breast cancer, a disease which did not then have the high profile it enjoys today, and became the founding patron of the Australian Breast Cancer Foundation. The second was the Australian fashion industry, to which she applied not only her European enthusiasm but also her name to various fashion scholarships. She even, uncharacteristically, posed for the front cover of *Vogue*, her distinctively wild hair tamed for the shoot.

Some described her as aloof, others commended her as the perfect prime ministerial wife. She describes herself as having a 'naturally reserved' manner, one that did not eclipse her husband's fame but rather complemented beautifully his image and his political aims. She was a poster girl for multicultural Australia and her command of languages helped Australia diplomatically. Some say she played a major part in securing the 2000 Olympic Games for Sydney.

Above: Annita and Paul celebrate Labor's election victory in 1993.
Left: Annita with one of her own photographs in 2004.

Annita stayed in Canberra after Labor's 1996 election defeat so the children could finish school, and eventually the couple began to spend less and less time together. Paul based himself in Sydney at their Woollahra mansion, in early 1998 the couple split. The media insinuations were that Annita was to blame, even though neither party ever publicly spoke about their reasons for the separation. Later that year she and the children moved to Sydney and lived without him.

The couple asked the media to respect their privacy. Without any first-hand explanation Paul was portrayed as the hapless victim and Annita as the one who was relieved to be free of the marriage. Despite the media glare, Annita began to construct her own life and completed a photography degree with distinction at the National Art School in Sydney. She has since gone on to do a Masters. She continues to be involved in causes she feels passionately about—such as the Spirit of the Land Foundation, a cross-cultural Aboriginal organisation that aims 'To build bridges of understanding between the indigenous and western cultures of the world.'

Sharon Arden-Osbourne

Married to Black Sabbath rocker Ozzie Osbourne, Sharon once said she 'lived 50 lives in 50 years' and she wasn't wrong. Sharon Osbourne is mother, wife, Emmy Award-winning producer, script writer and cancer survivor.

SHARON RACHEL ARDEN was born on 9 October 1952 in London. She was the daughter of rock and roll entrepreneur Don Arden and Hope. It's been well documented that Sharon didn't like her mother—she didn't attend her funeral in 1998. Sharon was thrown into the music industry when she was just 15, working for her dad as a receptionist at his artists' management company. It was there she first met Ozzy Osbourne, lead singer in her father's band, Black Sabbath.

Friends at first, Sharon was just 17 when they met, but the pair's relationship grew over several years. Sharon worked her way up from receptionist to managing two other bands herself—The Smashing Pumpkins and Coal Chamber, and briefly, Queen. In 1979 Ozzy was fired from Black Sabbath as he rarely turned up for gigs. Sharon took control of him at that point and guided him through a successful solo career. Sharon's faith and support in Ozzy caused a huge rift with her father and she bought out Ozzy's contract from her him.

Sharon and Ozzy were married on 4 July 1982 in Hawaii—despite her cheating on him with his guitarist Randy Rhoads who she said was there when she and Ozzy weren't speaking. The couple stayed in love and Sharon gave birth to three children—Aimee, Kelly and Jack born in the late 1980s. Ozzy was constantly on tour and Sharon made news for taking her children on tour as well—refusing to let anyone else mind them while they were growing up. It is rumoured that the tour bus was often used as a nursery.

At the same time, she juggled her international company, Sharon Osbourne Management, ran two record labels and became a film and concert producer. In 1996 she created Ozzfest, which still runs today. Headlined by Ozzy, Ozzfest tours various countries and brings new talent to the attention of the world.

While Ozzy remains a rocker, Sharon is always reinventing herself. She approached MTV about her idea for a television show, a fly-on-the-wall reality show called *The Osbournes*. Stepping

out from behind the camera, the show gave Sharon the coverage to become a celebrity in her own right. Since then, Sharon has had every TV station and magazine editor knocking on her door. She was featured in *Vanity Fair*, *Rolling Stone* and *People* magazines and was watched by millions on the show of US chat host Barbara Walters. People began to admire Sharon for her honesty, her skills as a patient wife and caring mother, while juggling her hugely successful show as well. While Ozzy was sitting in the living room inebriated, it was Sharon holding up the rest of the family. She was given her own show, *The Sharon Osbourne Show*, but this wasn't as popular on MTV as *The Osbournes* and was soon taken off air. She also judged UK talent show *The X Factor*.

The strength of her character and her determination to survive were tested when in July 2000, she was diagnosed with colon cancer. Later she announced the cancer had spread to her lymph nodes and she was more seriously ill than she—and everyone else—had thought. She underwent chemotherapy—and still allowed the TV cameras in for *The Osbournes*. She won her cancer battle against a 33 per cent survival prognosis. She dumped the band The Smashing Pumpkins in 2000 releasing a statement that said: 'I must resign due to medical reasons … Billy Corgan was making me sick!'

In August 2004 she founded the Sharon Osbourne Colon Cancer Foundation at Cedars Sinai Hospital in America and a mission to provide free screenings and healthcare to people that can't afford it. She wrote a bestseller, *Extreme* about her life which hit number one on the UK Bestseller List for six weeks in October 2005. The public love Sharon's honesty—she has admitted to having thousands of dollars worth of plastic surgery—and her positive approach to life has made her one of rock music's most successful figures.

Hillary Rodham Clinton

Hillary Rodham Clinton achieved a fame all of her own during her husband Bill's US Presidency from 1993 to 2001. A brilliant lawyer and speaker, she drafted health-care reforms and campaigned for the rights of children. What will Hillary do next?

BORN IN 1947 IN CHICAGO, HILLARY RODHAM spent her early life as she would her years as First Lady and, later, in the Senate—studying, speaking and leading her peers. Her upbringing was middle-class, with her father Hugh's textile business providing for his wife, daughter and two sons. In her school days, Hillary was active in the Methodist church as a youth leader. Her choice of college was the all-girl Wellesley College in Massachusetts, where she studied political science, became president of the student body and was involved in literacy programs for underprivileged children. In her late teens she was active in the Young Republicans, but the assassinations of Bobby Kennedy and Martin Luther King in the late 1960s were a political turning point, causing her to switch her allegiance to the Democratic Party. Her 1969 graduation speech tackled some controversial issues and gained nationwide coverage when it was published in *Life* magazine.

In 1971 at Yale Law School Hillary met Bill Clinton. She had noticed him the year before, but one day they were both in the law library. 'I noticed that he kept looking over at me. He had been doing a lot of that. So I stood up from the desk, walked over to him and said, "If you're going to keep looking at me, and I'm going to keep looking back, we might as well be introduced. I'm Hillary Rodham." That was it'. Some months later Hillary caught a bad cold, and Bill turned up at her door bearing chicken soup and orange juice. Not long after, they 'became inseparable', as Hillary puts it. At the end of their time at Yale, Bill returned to his native Arkansas, and Hillary stayed in the east to work for the Children's Defense Fund and the House Judiciary Committee working for the impeachment of President Nixon. In 1974, Hillary joined Bill in Arkansas and began teaching at the University of Arkansas School of Law.

Hillary married Bill in 1975 and joined a prominent law firm in Little Rock, later becoming a partner. While Bill served two terms as governor of Arkansas, Hillary not only maintained her position at the law firm, but worked on programs to help children and served on several boards

of large corporations. Their only child, Chelsea, was born in 1980, and Hillary was named Arkansas Mother of the Year in 1983. When political commentators questioned her commitment to her husband because she had retained her maiden name, she began calling herself Hillary Rodham Clinton.

In the 1992 presidential campaign, she was the first wife of an American presidential candidate to have her own strong political interests and a well-defined career that she seemed to have no intention of giving up. She acted as Bill's campaign adviser; she gave speeches and greeted voters; and she created a furore when, tired of the scrutiny about her career, she told a reporter she 'could have stayed at home, baked cookies, and had teas'. Some applauded her championing of women's work choices, but others claimed her comment showed her disrespect for women who had chosen to be homemakers. Hillary clarified her position and in the process learned a valuable lesson about the media—and she made sure she was not open to such criticism again.

When Bill became President in 1993, Hillary took an office in the West Wing of the White House—unheard of for a First Lady—and set about leading a task force to draft a comprehensive health-care reform package. While its recommendations were defeated in Congress, the proposed reforms received widespread praise. Her longstanding interest in children's rights continued, and her 1995 book *It Takes a Village: And Other Lessons Children Teach Us*, which focused on the problems facing children and families in modern American society, was a bestseller.

Hillary said in 1996, 'My husband and I have been best friends and partners for a very long time. We work together. We support each other ... I'm going to be there for him.' Two years later, this claim would be thoroughly tested.

In 1998, Bill testified that he had not had an affair with a young White House intern named Monica Lewinsky. Hillary publicly declared that she believed him, but two days before he was to give testimony before a grand jury he confessed to her that he and Lewinsky had in fact been sexually involved. 'As a wife, I wanted to wring Bill's neck', Hillary later said in her memoir, *Living History*, where she recalls that she could hardly breathe, was gulping for air and started crying and yelling at him, asking, 'Why did you lie to me?' But she chose to support him and stood by her husband during the extremely public and humiliating impeachment proceedings against him. The impeachment was unsuccessful, and the Clintons saw out the final months of the presidency. Hillary said, 'I had to ask myself whether I would continue to stay married or not—whether I could under those circumstances. And that was a very hard decision.'

Hillary was elected Senator for New York in November 2000. Even if Hillary herself has not confirmed her candidacy for president, if she does run for president, her familiarity with living a life under the gaze of the public will be one of her greatest assets.

Cherie Blair

Cherie Blair juggles her legal career with four children and her marriage to the British prime minister, Tony Blair. Some media gaffes have lost her some friends, but her profile as a high-powered working mother has put her in a league of her own—not least with her last child, Leo, who spent his first days in Downing Street as Cherie turned 45.

CHERIE BOOTH WAS BORN IN 1954 into a working class Catholic family in Lancashire in the north of England. Her father, Tony Booth, an actor, walked out on the family when Cherie was two. Cherie and her sister Lyndsey were brought up by their mother Gale and paternal grandmother Vera Booth. Cherie was bright at school and studied at the prestigious London School of Economics. She studied law and came top of her year in the bar exams.

Cherie met Tony Blair, one year her junior, while they were both training to be barristers. In 1976, at 22, she became a barrister. Four years later, in 1980, she married Tony. This was the era of Margaret Thatcher, prime minister from 1979 to 1990. Battling to get the Labour Party in power and turn back the economic rationalist agenda, Cherie and Tony were in the mainstream of Labour campaigning politics. Coming from a working class background, Cherie has always been an active supporter of the Labour Party. She attempted her own political career by fighting, but losing, the seat of Thanet North in Kent in the 1983 British general election. In the same year Tony won his safe seat in Sedgefield, County Durham, and began his long climb to government.

As the Blairs began their own family, and Cherie gave birth to Euan, Nicky and Kathryn, the pace of their political and working lives increased. In 1994, Tony was elected the youngest ever leader of the Labour Party, aged 41, and in 1997 became Prime Minister.

Tony Blair's new 'modern' Labour Party and his 'modern' working wife made the pair immediately attractive to the media. Cherie was a modern party leader's partner, representing working mothers who chose not to end their careers in the face of housework and childcare. The party's policies to secure government included a campaign to get more women MPs into parliamentary seats.

Despite the pressures of becoming the country's 'first lady', Cherie continued to develop her own career and in 1995 was appointed a Queen's Counsel (QC). In 1999 she was appointed a Recorder (a permanent part-time judge) in the County Court and Crown Court. She was a founding member,

Cherie Blair on a tour to Pakistan.

in 2000, of Matrix Chambers, London, from which she continues to practise as a barrister. Cherie, who works under her maiden name, specialises in employment, discrimination and public law and in this capacity has sometimes represented claimants taking cases against the UK government.

Many people see Cherie Blair as the UK's equivalent to Hillary Clinton, as partners of non-right wing leaders. Both were embroiled in scandal in their roles as first ladies in connection with their work. Cherie Booth hit the newspaper headlines in the 'Cheriegate' scandal because of her involvement with Peter Foster, a convicted Australian conman, who assisted her with the purchase of two flats in Bristol. Cherie tried to distance herself from Foster and briefed the press office at No 10 to go public with a statement claiming that Foster was not involved with the deal. She was caught out when Foster provided evidence that she had lied. She then went public herself, tearfully reading a prepared statement blaming her 'misfortune' on the pressures of running a family and being a working mother. But while Hillary battled her husband's affair with Monica Lewinsky, Cherie's marriage has always appeared stable, and in 1999 she gave birth to her fourth child, Leo, at the age of 45. Even as she brought a new baby home to Downing Street—the first one in 150 years—she did not noticeably slow down. She worked to the end of her pregnancy, appearing in court for the Trades Union Council in a case against the government. Her mothering skills then became the focus of intense media interest. When would she return to work? Would she insist Tony took parental leave? Would her mother move in to help? Would she opt for cloth nappies or disposables?

In 2005 Tony Blair, aged 52, won an historic third term of government—the only Labour Party leader to have won three elections in a row—with a reduced majority.

Cherie and her children remain in Downing Street. She lectures widely on human rights. She is Chancellor and Honorary Fellow of Liverpool John Moores University, Governor and Honorary Fellow of the London School of Economics and the Open University, a Fellow of the Royal Society of Arts, an Honorary Fellow of the Institute of Advanced Legal Studies, a Doctor of Laws (Westminster University) and a Fellow of the International Society of Lawyers for Public Service. Cherie also is involved extensively with charities. She is President of Barnardo's children's charity, a Trustee of Refuge and Vice-President of Family Mediators Association. She is also Patron of Breast Cancer Care, Sargent Cancer Care for Children and Victim Support London.

There have been many rumours about her running for parliament, but Cherie has denied them.

Jemima Khan

Before marrying Pakistani cricketing legend Imran Khan in 1995, Jemima Goldsmith was famous for simply being the rich, beautiful daughter of a billionaire. But after her marriage it was her tireless humanitarian work, embracing of Islam and brief but well-received foray into fashion design that gave her a public profile and fame of her own.

JEMIMA GOLDSMITH was born in 1974 to wealthy British—French businessman Sir James Goldsmith and Lady Annabel Stewart. In her youth Jemima was bright, beautiful and a particularly talented horsewoman—it was once predicted that the young heiress would go on to compete in showjumping. Her family moved in the upper echelons of British society, and Jemima's friends on the exclusive London social circuit included Princess Diana. Ultimately she enrolled at Bristol University to study English.

In 1993, during her university years, she met Imran Khan at a London nightclub. He was 42, and had a reputation for flamboyant playboy behaviour—and, at the same time, a commitment to the Islamic religion. Jemima was 21 and part-Jewish. The cultural and age differences didn't seem to bother the couple—they were married in 1995, at a brief ceremony conducted in Urdu, then at a civil ceremony in London. At the wedding party afterwards, Jemima requested that, instead of giving gifts, guests donate to the cancer hospital Imran had established in Lahore: the Shaukat Khanum Memorial Cancer Hospital and Research Centre, named after his mother.

This marked the beginning of Jemima's work as a campaigner for humanitarian and political causes, both alongside her husband and on her own. Relocating to Pakistan after her marriage, she learned to speak Urdu, converted to Islam and became known as Haiqa Khan. Jemima denied that she had been pressured into her conversion to Islam, telling the press, 'My conversion was not, as so many have assumed, a pre-requisite to my marriage. It was entirely my own choice.' She publicly refuted the perception that Islamic women are not permitted to play a role in public life, pointing out that Imran's own sisters led very public and successful lives in Pakistan and abroad.

While Imran became more politically focused, establishing, and campaigning with his party Tehrik-e-Insaaf (Movement for Justice), Jemima embarked on one of her first social campaigns—for improved literacy programs in Pakistan. She also turned her hand to business, first setting up

Jemima and Imran leave the registry office in London after their second wedding ceremony.

a tomato sauce enterprise, then embarking on the more successful 'Jemima Khan' fashion label, which had London fashion commentators in a flutter. Her women's clothing range used traditional Pakistani embroidery and the designs of the shalwar kameez—an elegant style of Islamic women's clothing consisting of pants and a skirt—and all her profits went to Imran's cancer hospital.

Jemima and Imran had two sons—Suleiman, born in 1996, and Qasim, born in 1999. But life wasn't easy for Jemima, who divided her time between Pakistan and London. While Imran was carving out a political career—he was finally elected to parliament in 2004—his political enemies often turned on Jemima who, was neither a Pakistani nor a Muslim by birth. In 1999, she was accused of trying to smuggle Pakistani antiques over to England. The rumour was vehemently denied by both Imran and Jemima, who claimed it was an attempt to weaken Imran's position in the eyes of the public. As Jemima told the British press, 'We are fed up with this constant victimisation.' In 2003 her London home was burgled and her bodyguard was stabbed. It was also claimed that she had become the target for Islamic terrorists.

During this tumultuous time, however, Jemima continued to further many humanitarian causes. In 2001 she ran a very public campaign to help Afghan refugees displaced by the 'war on terror'. In two weeks she raised $120 000 to buy tents for families living in refugee camps. In the same year, she became a UNICEF ambassador, fronting many global campaigns for the welfare of children. In 2003 she very publicly opposed America's invasion of Iraq. She championed Imran's political causes, even leading a 2002 protest in Islamabad against the actions of Israel and calling on the European Union to impose sanctions until Israel withdrew from Palestinian territories.

In 2003 Jemima moved back to London to study for a Master's degree. The following year Imran Khan announced that he and his wife had divorced after nine years of marriage. It was arranged that their children would divide their time between Pakistan and London. Despite the divorce, in 2005 Jemima undertook another campaign to help the victims of the earthquake in northern Pakistan alongside her ex-husband. 'I've been involved in promoting UNICEF work for victims of the earthquake, and also my ex-husband's appeal,' she declared at the time.

Imran blamed the break-up of their marriage on the pressures Jemima was under, saying that 'In the beginning the idea was that we would campaign together, but I had to pull her out of politics to shield her from it…That is when our problems began.'

Jemima has been mixing with high-profile names in the arts and entertainment world, and has been romantically linked to English actor Hugh Grant. In 2005 she announced that she would front UNICEF's campaign for children living with AIDS. 'I'll be involved with the campaign for as long as it takes,' she said. 'I feel passionately that I can make a lot of difference.'

Demi Moore

*Even Demi Moore would be the first to admit that her marriage in
1987 to actor Bruce Willis helped her find the kind of fame most
people only dream about. Since their separation and subsequent divorce
in 2000, Demi has continued to maintain her own brand of fame.*

SUCCESS WAS NOT SOMETHING THAT CAME NATURALLY to Demi Moore's family. Her father, Charles Harmon, left her mother, Virginia, before Demi was even born in 1962, in New Mexico. She grew up as Demetria Guynes, in the family of her stepfather Danny. He was a salesman, and the family moved about 40 times before Demi struck out on her own. When she was 14, Demi discovered that Danny—by all accounts an aggressive, abusive man—was not her real father. Two years later, she left school to pursue a modelling career; a year after that, Danny committed suicide. Her mother spiralled into a life of drug and alcohol addiction, and for many years mother and daughter were estranged from one another.

Incredibly, Demi's life did not implode. She found enough modelling work to get by, and began a relationship with musician Freddy Moore. They married in 1980 when Demi was 18, a marriage that lasted four years. In 1981, she scored a role on the soap opera *General Hospital* and in her first feature film, *Choices*. Other small film roles followed, and her persistence paid off: in 1984 she was cast in *St Elmo's Fire*. After a troubled time during which she was told she would be fired from the film if she didn't deal with her cocaine habit, she managed to get clean and get her career back on track. She met actor Emilio Estevez on set, and they became engaged. At the premiere of one of his films, *Stakeout*, in 1987, Demi met the charismatic Bruce Willis.

Bruce had a reputation as an up-and-coming star who liked to party and had won accolades for his role in the television series *Moonlighting*. Their courtship lasted only four months—they were married in Las Vegas in 1987 and became one of the most incessantly followed celebrity couples in Hollywood. Their first daughter, Rumer, was born in 1988, and in the next two years Demi hit the career jackpot. The 1990s saw her appear in a string of well-known films including *Ghost*, *A Few Good Men*, *Indecent Proposal*, *Disclosure*, *The Scarlet Letter*, *Striptease* and *GI Jane*. Professionally, the couple was known to support each other, with Bruce even stripping on *The*

Demi, Bruce and the girls attend the Academy Awards in the 1990s.

David Letterman Show to promote Demi in *Striptease*. Demi was realistic about the relationship's chances of survival: 'The truth is you can have a great marriage, but there are still no guarantees'. But the marriage seemed to last, and they had two more daughters: Scout, born in 1991, and Tallulah, in 1994. In 1991, *Vanity Fair* published a nude photo of the seven-months-pregnant Demi on its cover. The following year she caused a similar stir by appearing in the same magazine wearing nothing more than body paint.

By the time Demi appeared in 1996's *GI Jane*, her career as an actress had reached its peak. She worked on the film as a producer, and attracted much criticism for her reportedly excessive demands behind the scenes. She rented a mansion, engaged a crowd of assistants and other staff, and even had two private jets at her disposal. Some film insiders referred to her as 'Gimme Moore', and her determination and toughness were widely known. Her marriage to Bruce was, however, on a downhill slide; a bitter (and very public) legal battle with one of their nannies, who made scandalous accusations about the couple's suitability as parents, didn't help. In 1998 they announced their separation, citing the pressures of the celebrity life. The divorce became official in 2000. Bruce bought a house just a few kilometres away from the family home in Hailey, Idaho, and he and Demi remained on good terms, appearing in public with their daughters and refusing to speak critically of one other to the media.

Demi returned to some smaller roles and worked as a producer on the *Austin Powers* trilogy. After five years of keeping a low profile, her position in the media spotlight was reignited when she started a relationship with actor Ashton Kutcher, who is 15 years her junior. At their wedding in October 2005, all three of Demi's children made speeches about their affection for 'MOD' (My Other Dad), as they called Ashton. Demi and Ashton sold the photos of their wedding to a magazine for US$3 million and said they were giving the money to charity. Bruce was also at the wedding, and made a speech suggesting that Ashton would have made him a perfect son-in-law— but showing his goodwill and continued closeness to his former wife.

The New Millennium
2000-

Winnie Mandela

Winnie Madikizela Mandela was once known as the Mother of the Nation, devoting her life to fighting the apartheid regime of South Africa. Imprisoned and harassed by police, she never gave up her support for her husband Nelson. Since his release her life has taken a difficult turn and she is struggling with the darker side of notoriety.

NOMZAMO NOBANDLA WINNIFRED MADIKIZELA was born the fourth of eight children on 26 September 1934. She was raised in Bizana, Transkei, a mountainous region on the south–east coast of South Africa, the ethnic home of the Xhosa tribe. Her mother was a domestic science teacher and died when Winnie was only eight years old. Her father was a head teacher at a mission school and later a minister of Forestry and Agriculture Department of the Transkei government during Kaiser Matanzima's rule.

Winnie went to Shawbury High School and completed a Social Work diploma at the Jan Hofmeyer School in Johannesburg, and then a Bachelor of Arts in Political Science with an International Relations major at the University of the Witwatersrand, in Johannesburg. When she became the first African medical social worker at a hospital, she came face to face with poverty and injustice.

'It was while working at Baragwanath Hospital that I started to become politicised,' she says on the African National Congress website. 'I started to realise the abject poverty under which most people were forced to live, the appaling conditions created by the inequalities of the system' ... Above all, I became politically conscious through the research I had carried out in Alexandra township to establish the rate of infantile mortality—it was 10 deaths in every 1000 births.'

In the early 1950s, the African National Congress began a campaign of defiance, using mass boycotts, strikes and civil disobedience, against the apartheid regime. It was during her involvement in this campaign that Winnie met Nelson Mandela, a 40-year-old attorney high up in the ranks of the ANC. Nelson was constantly on the move to avoid police arrest and harassment. Despite the difficult circumstances of their courtship, their relationship developed and they married in Bizana in 1958. It was not long before Winnie too was dodging arrest. Her first detention was in 1958, and coincided with the mass arrests of women involved in the anti-pass campaign. At the time, she was

the chairperson of the Orlando West branch of both the ANC and the ANC Women's League.

In 1959 Winnie gave birth to their first child, Zenani, and in 1961 their second daughter, Zindziswa, was born. Winnie and Nelson had only four years together before he was sentenced to life imprisonment on conspiracy charges in 1964. He was taken to the notorious Robben Island prison, 10 kilometres off the coast of Cape Town. Even before that he had been forced to live apart from his family, moving from place to place to evade detection by the government's ubiquitous informers and police spies. Over the years Mandela had adopted a number of disguises and his lengthy evasion of the police had earned him the title of the 'Black Pimpernel'.

'I know the pain of my people's suffering, the pain of having a husband behind bars for 25 years, the pain of bringing up children under the atmosphere I brought them up'

At the age of 30 Winnie was left alone with her two daughters, aged only four and five, and was only allowed to visit her husband every six months. The security forces recognised the significance of her political role and placed her under constant observation. She said on BBC Online: 'It was a day to day kind of existence. We were harassed from the moment their father was out of the picture. It was extremely difficult to explain to very young children why it was so, why I would be followed, if I was not a criminal.' Visiting her husband in prison was difficult. It wasn't until her daughters each turned 16 that they were allowed their first 'contact' visits to their father. A letter Nelson Mandela wrote to Winnie in 1979 from his Robben Island prison cell said: 'Had it not been for your visits, wonderful letters and your love, I would have fallen apart many years ago.'

On and off, all through the 1960s and 70s, Winnie was detained, placed in solitary confinement, placed under house arrest, imprisoned and exiled. She didn't give up campaigning, forming the Black Women's Federation, the Black Parents' Association and being active in the ANC Women's League.

Interviewed in 1986, she described the effect that years of harassment, solitary confinement and separation from her husband had had upon her. 'All I know is I am terribly brutalised inside. I know my soul is scarred, I know I am bleeding inside all the time. I know the pain of my people's suffering, the pain of having a husband behind bars for 25 years, the pain of bringing up children under the atmosphere I brought them up … But what has happened is that hasn't brutalised me to an extent of being consumed in hate.'

In 1985 she returned to Soweto to continue the struggle in defiance of the security forces. In the late 1980s, reports of the brutality of her personal bodyguards in Soweto, nicknamed the Mandela United Football Club, made Winnie a figure of controversy. Then in 1989, 14-year-old activist Stompei Seipei Moketsi, was kidnapped by her guards and later found murdered. The ANC leadership declared that she was out of control but Nelson Mandela refused to repudiate her.

In 1990, Nelson was released from prison after 28 years. The day of the release saw Winnie by his side and he held fast to his belief in her innocence. In 1991 Winnie was elected to the ANC's National Executive but in the same year was charged with the assault and kidnapping of Stompei. Convicted and given six years in jail, she appealed and the sentence was reduced to a fine.

In 1994 Nelson Mandela was elected President of South Africa and Winnie was elected to Parliament. She was given the post of Deputy Minister for Arts, Culture, Science and Technology in the new government but was sacked less than a year later for ignoring party discipline and for continued criticism of the government. At the time, Nelson Mandela said that he hoped the act of being sacked would help her to review and seek to improve her conduct.

But it was not to be. In 1996 the Mandelas went through a humiliating public divorce and in 1997 Winnie appeared before the Truth and Reconciliation Committee, where she had to defend herself against allegations of murder and assault. The TRC aimed to uncover the truth about human rights abuses under apartheid and to promote reconciliation through hearing the testimony of those who suffered and the confessions of torturers and terrorists. It concluded that she was aware of, and in some cases probably took part in, murders, abductions and assaults by the Mandela United Football Club. The commission's report also says she allowed her home to be used as a place for assault and mutilation.

Winnie continued in her role in the ANC Women's League and as a Member of Parliament but corruption raised its head again when she was convicted of fraud. In 2004, an appeal judge upheld a prison sentence handed down to her on 43 convictions of fraud, but suspended it for five years. She resigned her seat in Parliament and her positions as a member of the executive committee of the governing African National Congress and the head of the ANC Women's League. Haleh Afshar, Professor of Politics and Women's Studies at York University, summarises Winnie's achievements and acknowledges her shortcomings:

'Winnie Mandela is another example of woman in resistance [in] impossible situations because she represented her husband when he was unable to speak… and she stood for him, and she always spoke as if she were his voice. What is interesting, and what we saw once he came out, is that very often she was her own voice but she represented him because it was easier to represent a male voice in a male world. Winnie Mandela has suffered from her own vision of herself. She fought hard for many years, in impossible positions, and defended a cause that she believed in.'

These words echo those of magistrate, Peet Johnson: 'Only a fool would underplay the important role you played in our history,' he said. 'Somewhere it seems that something went wrong ...'

Graça Machel

An experienced political operator and a dedicated campaigner for equality, Graça Machel is also the only woman to become the First Lady of two different nations—Mozambique and South Africa. She is married to former president Nelson Mandela.

GRAÇA SIMBENE WAS BORN IN THE SOUTHERN PROVINCE OF GAZA in the African country Mozambique in October 1946. Many families were being forced by the country's Portuguese colonialists to grow cotton for profit rather than desperately needed food crops and hunger was prevalent in the rural areas. Few professions were open to Mozambican black men, let alone women. In the 1950s many farmers had their land confiscated and given to Portuguese settlers. To avoid starvation, the farmers went to work in the South African mines where dangerous conditions often ended in death.

Against this background, Graça went to Methodist Mission schools and stood out to win a scholarship to attend Lisbon University in Portugal, a rare achievement for a Mozambican woman. She became involved in independence campaigns to free the country from its colonial restraints. She finished her qualifications to become a school teacher and went back to Mozambique in 1973. There she joined the Mozambican Liberation Front (FRELIMO). By 1970, Samora Machel had become commander-in-chief of the FRELIMO army which had established itself among Mozambique's peasantry. The FRELIMO army had weakened colonial power and, after a coup in Portugal in 1974, the Portuguese left Mozambique. After electoral victory for FRELIMO, Mozambique won its independence in 1974.

Graça was a key figure in the struggle and was appointed the country's first Minister for Education and Culture in the new government, the only woman in the cabinet. She met and married the charismatic Samora Machel in 1975, taking on the five children from his first marriage to Jozina, a guerrilla fighter who had died in 1971 in the camps of Tanzania.

Machel became independent Mozambique's first president on 25 June, 1975. He called for the nationalisation of Portuguese plantations and property, and established government schools and health clinics for the peasants. The white regimes of Rhodesia (Zimbabwe) and South Africa tried

to sabotage his plans and the economy suffered. As education minister, Graça Machel oversaw an increase of Mozambique's school-going population from 400 000 to 1.6 million and gave birth to two children. On a stormy evening on 19 October, 1986, Samora Machel was on his way back from an international meeting in Malawi in the presidential Tupolev Tu-134 aircraft when the plane crashed in the Lebombo Mountains, near Mbuzini. There were nine survivors but President Machel and 24 others died, including ministers and officials of the Mozambique government. While there was widespread suspicion—both nationally and internationally—that the apartheid regime of South Africa was implicated in the crash, no conclusive evidence to this effect has yet emerged. Graça Machel is convinced the aircrash was no accident and has dedicated her life to tracking down her husband's killers. Her children have vowed to carry on the hunt.

After her retirement from the Mozambique ministry, Graça Machel produced the groundbreaking United Nations Report on the Impact of Armed Conflict on Children. She received the 1995 Nansen Medal from the United Nations in recognition of her longstanding humanitarian work, particularly on behalf of refugee children. The role of grieving widow was not to remain, for Graça was thrust back into the international spotlight when she began a relationship with Nelson Mandela, the President of South Africa. For years she refused to consider marrying him, partly due to pressure from the Machel family but also because of resistance from Mozambique's President Joachim Chissano. Finally, in July 1998 she changed her mind and married Madiba. She deleted the 'obey' from their ceremony and chose instead to love, honour and cherish him.

As South Africa's new first lady she was determined to continue her work in Maputo, where she runs her own children's foundation. The couple maintain residences in both South Africa and Mozambique. Samora Machel's presence is firmly entrenched in the giant black-and-white photograph of him that dominates the lounge of their Maputo residence. His death is still a traumatic subject for Graça.

Graça Machel is an intensely private person. She seldom gives public interviews and guards her personal life. Debora Patta's interview her her in the *Weekly Mail and Guardian* is one of the few in the public domain. Speaking about the aircrash with Patta at the Presidency with Nelson Mandela, Graça was reduced to tears—'tears that were gently wiped away by Madiba [Mandela]. Ever the dignified statesman, he responded to the situation with deep sensitivity and generously used the occasion to pay tribute to Samora Machel's leadership and vision as a true son of Africa.'

In a radio interview in 1996, Graça gave a rare insight into her emotional life: 'It's just wonderful that after so much pain I have gone through—and I believe that is also from Nelson's side—that finally we have found each other and can start to share a life together,' she said. 'There were times when I thought it couldn't happen any more in my life.'

Kirsty Sword-Gusmão

He was a rebel and a guerrilla leader who lived in the jungle; she was a foreign aid worker and undercover agent. Australian Kirsty Sword was thrown into the public spotlight when she married Xanana Gusmão and became first lady of East Timor.

Kirsty Sword grew up in the Melbourne suburb of Northcote. She had always been fascinated with Indonesia, and majored in Indonesian at Bendigo University. In her twenties she started to travel to Indonesia. In the 1980s she worked as a volunteer for *Inside Indonesia* magazine, reporting on human rights, the role of the Indonesian armed forces, and the plight of poor people. In Jakarta, where she worked as an English teacher, Kirsty began to get involved with the East Timorese resistance campaigns, helping young students involved in the pro-independence movement. Taking the codename Ruby Blade to protect her identity, Kirsty translated documents, drafted petitions and visited members of human rights delegations. She even helped smuggle seven East Timorese men to safety in a foreign consulate in Jakarta.

She described her role in *The Sunday Telegraph* magazine in 2002: 'I was a bit of a bridge between the different elements of the resistance inside East Timor and in Indonesia. Often it was really rather menial, getting documents from one place to another and doing it safely. I moved into it gradually. It was after I made contact with Xanana and he asked me to do things for him, that I realised that I was in pretty deep. Up until that time I had taken it as a bit of a side interest. After that it really did became the main thing in my life. I was deeply involved in the resistance long before I actually met Xanana.'

Xanana Gusmão was a freedom fighter sentenced to life imprisonment for leading the resistance against the government. He had been arrested and imprisoned in Jakarta in 1992 after almost 18 years living and fighting in the bush. Kirsty began to give Xanana English lessons via correspondence while smuggling in documents in and out of prison.

Kirsty also brought him materials that he used for his artwork—he loved to paint. In 1994, she sent Xanana a photograph of herself in some rice fields and he sent her back a painting he had done of the picture. They kept up the correspondence, sending gifts, paintings and letters, until

December 1994, when Kirsty turned up in the prison on the pretence of meeting someone else. They fell in love, even though Xanana was 20 years her senior and already married.

After Xanana was released from jail he divorced his wife and married Kirsty in July 2000. She gave birth to their son Alexandre two months later and they have since had two more sons.

Xanana was elected president of East Timor in 2002 and has been hailed a national hero for his work fighting for the freedom of the East Timorese people. Kirsty became first lady of the world's newest nation. A friend gave her a t-shirt with: 'Living with a saint is far more gruelling than being one.'

Along with the more traditional roles of that position—meeting and greeting international VIPs—she took on a heavy workload. She is the head and founder of the Alola Foundation, which supports women's issues, and is named after a 15 year-old girl who was kidnapped by a militia leader during the post-referendum violence in 1999 and forced to be one of his wives, where she remains today. Breastfeeding is another issue Kirsty is passionate about and in 2003 founded the National Breastfeeding Association of East Timor, to give much needed maternal and child health a boost. She has been compared to Hillary Clinton and has been called the Jackie O of the East, and the mother of the nation. East Timor's foreign minister described her as indispensable to the resistance movement and said she is; 'reliable, discreet, humble…That woman is perfect.' But Kirsty just retorts that she is a human being with a conscience. 'There is nothing heroic about responding when a group of people come to you and say, "this is out story, can you help us?" Once I started to get involved there was a tremendous gratification in actually being able to do something.'

Kirsty works in the office of the presidential home, a cluster of small bungalows at Balibur in the hills above the capital Dili, where she lives with Xanana, Alexandre, and a variety of helpers, volunteers, bodyguards and houseguests. Much of the affairs of state are carried out there. In the 2007 elections Xanana must decide whether he will stand again for a second term. 'Even if he doesn't run again, it's clear that both he and I will continue our roles in public life because we're in positions where we both can help,' says Kirsty.

They both need bodyguards and Kirsty has had to adjust living with them. She told the *Sunday Telegraph*, 'It took a lot of getting used to. I am a very independent person who values being able to be spontaneous. I like to jump in my car and drive to just clear my head but I can't do that any more. It's a whole new way of approaching your life.'

'We have fantasised in the last couple of years about what it could be like if he had managed to avoid this fate of being president. We would like to travel around East Timor as ordinary citizens, and paint and draw and write. Grow pumpkins. We have cows, but they don't actually live with us. They were donated to us and they are being cared for until as we find a plot of land.'

Marion Jones

American athletics star Marion Jones became the first woman to win five track and field medals at a single Olympics in 2000. Her early marriage to world champion shot-putter CJ Hunter gave her a public profile before she made her name on the world stage, and her later relationship with sprinter Tim Montgomery caused even more of a sensation.

IT WAS WATCHING THE 1984 OLYMPICS, and particularly the performances of flamboyant track star Florence Griffith-Joyner, that inspired the nine-year-old Marion Jones to become an Olympian. She showed early promise, and her family moved around so that she could be part of the best high school track teams. In 1992, aged 17, she won a place as a reserve in the US Olympic team, but decided instead to concentrate on basketball. She won a basketball scholarship with the University of North Carolina, studying journalism. Foot injuries and basketball commitments prevented her from trying out for the 1996 Olympic team, but she returned once again to training for the track after she graduated in 1997.

At university she met world champion shot-putter CJ Hunter. He was working as a coach for the track team, and was seven years older than Marion. When their relationship was discovered, the head coach forced CJ to choose between Marion and his job. He chose Marion, and they married in 1998. CJ was a big man, known as much for his aggression and temper as his shot-putting ability. Just before the Sydney Olympics, he failed a drug test and retired from the sport, apparently telling his wife it was because of a knee injury. In her autobiography, Marion claims she was shocked: 'He kept the truth from me. It's possible he flat-out lied ... I was his wife! I trusted him.'

The year 2000 was Marion's year. Although her marriage was disintegrating and her name had become associated with CJ's drugs controversy, her performance at the Olympics was spectacular. She won three gold medals (100 m, 200 m and 4 x 400 m relay) and two bronze medals (long jump and 4 x 100 m relay), becoming the first woman to win so many medals in track and field

Marion Jones and CJ Hunter in Sydney in 2000.

events at a single Olympics. And something else started happening at those Olympics, too—it's said that a romance was building between Marion and fellow athlete Tim Montgomery.

In 2001, Marion and CJ separated, but she continued to shine, winning two events at the 2001 World Championships. She was again successful in the 2002 athletics season. By mid-year her relationship with Tim was finally made public. They moved in together in Raleigh, North Carolina, and became training partners. They quickly became a celebrity sports couple—with Marion as its more famous half. When Tim broke the world record in the 100 m in 2002, he dedicated his achievement to Marion. When asked about how he managed to break the record, he attributed it to his relationship: 'When your heart is at ease, your mind is at ease'. Despite the media attention, Marion seemed happy, too: 'We're both quite aware we are public figures and we respect that. We would just hope that everybody would respect the fact we have our private lives ... We're just very happy'.

It seemed controversy could not leave such a high-profile couple alone for long. They dumped their coach and started training with Charlie Francis, best known for working with sprinter Ben Johnson when he failed a drug test and was stripped of his 100m world record after the 1988 Olympics. This drew harsh criticism from the press, and Marion and Tim were forced to publicly explain their decision to change coaches. A happier event in 2003 was the birth of their son, Timothy (known as 'Monty'). As Marion said at the time, 'I am so happy. This is the greatest thing that has ever happened to me. He's a beautiful baby and Tim and I could not be more excited.' She leapt back into training, but despite hopes for a comeback, her performances in the trials for the Athens Olympics in 2004 were disappointing. She qualified in the long jump, but only finished fifth. Tim failed to qualify at all. It seemed that their relationship was becoming strained.

'We decided to remain friends so we can concentrate on making a future for our two-year-old son.'

At the end of 2004, the scandal broke that would change their lives. Both Tim and Marion were accused of using performance-enhancing drugs, although neither of them had ever failed a drug test. The accusation was made by a pharmaceutical company, Balco Laboratories, which was being investigated for supplying undetectable drugs to athletes. Tim and Marion fervently denied it. Other athletes waded into the controversy, including CJ Hunter, who claimed he had watched—and helped—Marion inject a range of drugs, including human growth hormone and an undetectable drug called 'the clear', at the time of the Sydney Olympics. Marion's lawyers acted swiftly, filing a US$25 million lawsuit for defamation against CJ, and claiming that he was bitter about the end of their marriage.

The accusations against Marion have not been officially proved. In December 2005, the evidence from Balco and from fellow athletes suggesting Tim had used drugs was accepted. He was banned for two years from competition, with all his performances from 2001 onwards to be disregarded, including his 2002 world record (although it had since been broken). When the decision came through, Tim announced that was retiring and that Marion and he had split up. Tim blamed their break-up on the pressure of the drugs scandal: 'It's kind of hard to be underneath the same household when you are going through some of the same things. We decided to remain friends so we can concentrate on making a future for our two-year-old son.' Marion herself has so far been silent.

Marion Jones' achievements in track and field made her better known than both her Olympian partners. She faces an uncertain future in the media-hyped arena of elite sport, and it remains to be seen whether she can emerge with her reputation intact.

Nicole Kidman

Nicole Kidman's marriage to the very high-profile actor Tom Cruise catapulted her further into the media limelight. Her painful divorce has seen her move to greater heights as an actress.

Nicole Kidman was born in Honolulu, Hawaii, on 20 June 1967 into a middle-class wealthy family. Her father, Dr Anthony Kidman, was a cancer specialist. When she was four Dr Kidman accepted a job as lecturer at the University of Technology in Sydney and they moved back to Australia. Nicole's love for performing arts was evident from a young age. She learned ballet from the age of four and studied at St Martin's Youth Theatre in Melbourne, and in Sydney at the Australian Theatre for Young People and the Philip Street Theatre, where she majored in voice production and theatre history.

When her mother, Janelle, was diagnosed with breast cancer, Nicole dropped out of all her studies to help look after her. She was just 17 and said later that what her mother went through will be 'imprinted' in her memory forever.

She first gained notice as a 16-year-old for her performance in *Bush Christmas* (1983), a film that became a holiday perennial on Australian television, and won acclaim for her work in the mini-series *Vietnam* (1985). *BMX Bandits* soon followed, as did a role in the TV soap opera *A Country Practice*. In 1989 she appeared in the successful thriller *Dead Calm* with Billy Zane and Sam Neill. At this point, movie buffs in America sat up and took notice.

Nicole met American actor Tom Cruise while starring opposite him in the 1990 movie *Days Of Thunder*. Despite Tom being married to Mimi Rogers, they fell in love. After Tom and Mimi divorced, he and Nicole married in December 1990. Tom said at the time: 'My first reaction to meeting Nic was pure lust. It was totally physical. I thought she was amazingly sexy and stunning.'

During her 10-year marriage, Nicole continued to work, yet her roles were overshadowed by Tom and his career. They lived around the world, in Los Angeles, Sydney and Byron Bay, Colorado and New York City. She enjoyed a solid reputation in Australia, but not in America. They made two other movies together— Stanley Kubrick's *Eyes Wide Shut* and Ron Howard's *Far And Away*, and Nicole swore she would never again make another movie with her husband again for fear of

wrecking her marriage. By then they were Hollywood's Golden Couple and were pictured on the covers of magazines worldwide. They adopted two children—Isabella and Conor.

It wasn't until 2001, when Tom and Nicole sensationally divorced, that the world began to really appreciate Nicole's talent. It has never been clear why the couple broke up. One persistent rumour claims that Nicole was not supportive of Tom's Scientology beliefs and wanted to bring up their children as Catholics.

Despite her obvious depression at their split, combined with a distressing miscarriage to Tom, Nicole threw herself into her work. By far her most successful year was 2001: she won an Academy Award for her performance in *Moulin Rouge*, her role in the horror film *The Others* was noted and she was also nominated for a Golden Globe for *The Others*. She won another Academy Award for her portrayal of Virginia Woolf in *The Hours* in 2003, as well as a Golden Globe, BAFTA and various other critic's awards.

Nicole and Tom in Sydney in 1993.

In August 2004, the Australian magazine *BRW* listed her as the richest Australian woman under the age of 40, with an estimated worth of A\$155 million, and she was listed 45th Most Powerful Celebrity on the 2005 Forbes Celebrity 100 List.

Nicole has been Goodwill Ambassador for UNICEF since 1994, and works hard to raise money and highlight the plight of disadvantaged children in Australia and the rest of the world. She supports Australian theatre and the film industry and has begun several projects with fellow Australian Russel Crowe. In 2004 she was honoured as a Citizen of the World by the United Nations and in January 2006 she was made a Companion in the general division of the Order of Australia for her services to performing arts. The award also recognised her dedication to health care through contributions to help improve treatment for women and children and her advocacy of cancer research.

Since her split with Tom she has dated rock and roll singer Lenny Kravitz and is set to marry country and western singer Keith Urban. Nicole has remained tight-lipped about her love life. 'Unless I'm married, I don't talk about it. It's that simple. I can't. It's not being coy; it's being protective—of my own emotions and protective of any person in my life. And my children.'

Crown Princess Mary of Denmark

When Tasmanian commoner Mary Donaldson met Crown Prince Frederik of Denmark in a Sydney bar in 2000, her life was set to change. 'Our Mary' became a Danish princess. Along the way she has had to step into the media glare that comes with the job.

Mary Elizabeth Donaldson was born in 1972 in Hobart, Tasmania, the youngest of four children. Her parents, John and Henrietta, emigrated from the UK to Australia in 1963, becoming Australian citizens. Their children were all born in Australia. Mary was educated in the Tasmanian public school system in Hobart and graduated from the University of Tasmania in 1994 with a Bachelor's degree in Commerce and Law. After completing postgraduate certificates in advertising and marketing, Mary worked in advertising in Melbourne. After her mother died in 1997, Mary took a year-long working holiday to the United States and Europe, returning in 1999.

During the Sydney Olympics in September 2000, Mary was socialising with friends at an inner Sydney bar, the Slip Inn. Her group fell in with a group of visiting Europeans. She began chatting to a friendly Dane, Frederik, who was accompanying the Danish sailing team. As Mary tells it, 'Half an hour after we first met, my then flatmate said, "These are actually European royalty that we're with". So I knew that he was a prince after about half an hour.' They got along well enough for Mary to give Frederik her phone number—for both of them, something had 'clicked'. He phoned her the next day.

They kept in touch when Frederik returned to Denmark, maintaining a long-distance relationship, and in 2001 Mary made her first visit to Denmark, prompting the Danish press to report that a 'mystery woman' had stolen Frederik's heart. But unless they wanted to keep living on opposite sides of the world, one of them would have to move. It was Mary who relocated, first to London, then to Copenhagen in late 2002 where she took a job as project consultant with

Microsoft. The Danish media went into a frenzy and apparently hired private investigators to put her under constant surveillance—they even sorted through her garbage to discover her identity. This was Mary's first taste of the lengths the Danish press would go to for 'news' relating to the royal family—and the first hint that the soon-to-be princess would be a figure of fascination for the people of her new home country.

The press didn't have to wait long for official news of a royal wedding. On a trip to Rome, Frederik proposed to Mary. As he tells it, 'I thought, "This is the moment. Seize the day and ... get your kneepads on."' In October 2003, their engagement was announced by Queen Margrethe, Frederik's mother. The scrutiny on the royal couple intensified—particularly on Mary as she was a foreigner and a commoner. Would she be able to live up the expectations of a royal house established over 1000 years ago?

The couple's wedding in May 2004 was a traditional and elegant royal event, attracting huge crowds in Copenhagen and more than a million viewers in Australia for each of its two televised screenings. The prince and princess honeymooned privately in Africa and returned to Denmark. For Mary, learning the Danish language was now even more crucial as most of her official meetings would now be conducted in Danish, and her studies intensified. She became the patron of many cultural and social organisations, focusing on causes for children and health, including mental health. As Mary told *Vogue* magazine, 'There is a lot to weigh up, but my biggest hope is to be able to make a difference somewhere. It's a privilege to have this opportunity.'

Within weeks of their wedding came rumours and speculation over when the couple would produce an heir. 'Is she, or isn't she?' pregnancy stories were constantly reported in the Danish press: when Mary had her gall bladder removed in hospital, the speculation was rife—was she having an ultrasound? Was that a pregnancy she was concealing? As Mary commented, 'I could not believe ... what the press could write'—fame obviously had its unpleasant side. The stories continued during Mary and Frederik's official tour of Australia in early 2005, where they attended charity events for Save the Children, Red Cross, the Victor Chang Foundation and other causes.

Soon the press were able to announce Mary's pregnancy, and despite a few panicked media reports of prenatal problems, Mary gave birth in October 2005 to Christian. Now Mary is not only the crown princess, but mother of the next heir to the Danish throne after her husband. Frederik has shown nothing but support for his wife as she negotiates the new situations that he has become familiar with during his life as the crown prince: 'It's quite impressive, what she's currently doing and has done already. I can only praise that'.

Seemingly at home in her new role, Princess Mary has made a remarkable start to a very public life as Australia's home-grown princess.